MW01265268

Nothing Gray About It

Emotional Purity Before a Holy God

Irene Sposato

WESTBOW·
PRESS
A DIVISION OF THOMAS NELSON
& ZONDERVAN

Graphics/art by Kupendwa Ministries

Scripture taken from the Holy Bible, NEW INTERNATIONAL VERSION®.
Copyright © 1973, 1978, 1984 by Biblica, Inc. All rights reserved worldwide.
Used by permission. NEW INTERNATIONAL VERSION® and NIV® are
registered trademarks of Biblica, Inc. Use of either trademark for the offering
of goods or services requires the prior written consent of Biblica US, Inc.

WestBow Press books may be ordered through booksellers or by contacting:

WestBow Press
A Division of Thomas Nelson & Zondervan
1663 Liberty Drive
Bloomington, IN 47403
www.westbowpress.com
1 (866) 928-1240

Because of the dynamic nature of the Internet, any web addresses or
links contained in this book may have changed since publication and
may no longer be valid. The views expressed in this work are solely those
of the author and do not necessarily reflect the views of the publisher,
and the publisher hereby disclaims any responsibility for them.

Any people depicted in stock imagery provided by Thinkstock are
models, and such images are being used for illustrative purposes only.
Certain stock imagery © Thinkstock.

ISBN: 978-1-4908-5470-0 (sc)
ISBN: 978-1-4908-5471-7 (hc)
ISBN: 978-1-4908-5469-4 (e)

Library of Congress Control Number: 2014917623

Printed in the United States of America.

WestBow Press rev. date: 10/17/2014

To my precious daughter,
who kept my secret for a year and a half.
May you always guard your heart …

Above all else, guard your heart,
for it is the wellspring of life.
Put away perversity from your mouth;
keep corrupt talk far from your lips.
Let your eyes look straight ahead,
fix your gaze directly before you.
Make level paths for your feet
and take only ways that are firm.
Do not swerve to the right or the left;
keep your foot from evil.

—Proverbs 4:23–27

Contents

Acknowledgments

As a woman who in her wildest dreams never thought she would write a book, I am indebted and eternally grateful to some incredible people.

To my husband, Chris, you truly are one of a kind. You read, edited, reread, edited again, and finally said, "I think you need a woman to read this." Thank you for spending hours editing when your own plate was full. Thank you for believing in me when I doubted myself. I truly love you, and there is no one I would rather share life with.

Jennifer Lazo, you were the "woman" who read this. You read and edited, offering nothing but encouragement and inspiration. I still remember your words when you first told me, "I'm so proud of you." You constantly kept me on track, reminding me where to keep my focus. You steer me toward holiness and are my pencil sharpener. Every woman deserves a BFF like you, and I'm so grateful you are mine.

Suzanne Comparato, you also were another woman who read this. You flew here through snow and ice to read the entire manuscript in three days. You are a rock. Your commitment to your marriage is a model for all of us. Thank you for teaching me about the sanctity of marriage. You gave me a necklace that weaves all the pieces of this book beautifully together, much as our lives are interwoven.

To my parents, you love me unconditionally. Thank you for always supporting and always being available; I couldn't ask for better parents. *Minä rakastan sinua.*

To Heather Kirby and Alison Norris, you are sweet friends. Both of you are beautiful inside and out. Heather, you are such an inspiration to me through your genuineness. You are as real as one can be. I admire your heart, which seeks no recognition or fanfare. Alison, you have taught me many things. You are a living example of the gospel. Thank you for teaching me to love others through God's eyes, for it is the kindness of God that leads us to repentance.

To Denise Weimer, you have become a good friend, and you are also a gifted writer. I am so thankful for your friendship, words of wisdom, time, and willingness to always help me. I know our paths crossed at just the right time.

To Suzanne Chambers, you were the first one I approached with a very rough draft in hand. You told me I wasn't crazy and that women do struggle with emotional purity. Even though I felt foolish, you affirmed me. You are a gifted teacher who has taught me the value of investing in eternal things.

To Stephanie Woelfl, you read what I thought was a final draft and inspired me to be better. Thank you for encouraging me to write a Bible study and believing in it with me.

To many other lovely friends who didn't even know I was writing, thank you for your friendship and your relentless pursuit of holiness in the ways you live your lives. Your fingerprints are all over this.

To Kupendwa Ministries, thank you for allowing me the privilege of sharing your story. I believe in it and want others to invest in this "true reality."

Introduction

When I moved to Georgia several years ago, one thing struck me besides the beautiful hardwood trees and the change of seasons. It was the fireplaces. I'm not referring to the traditional fireplaces inside of homes, but fireplaces outside in the middle of nowhere. There are fireplaces on open farmland where cattle graze, fireplaces hidden at entrances to housing communities, and even fireplaces cleverly disguised on golf courses. They stand tall and forgotten by what once surrounded them.

Several years after my move, I had the opportunity to ask a longtime resident of our community what purpose the remaining fireplaces served. I rationalized that someone who had been born and raised here would surely know the answer to my question. Unfortunately, she had no idea. I wasn't prepared for what she said next. She said she had not even noticed the fireplaces and asked where I had seen them. Let me assure you, they are everywhere in this part of the woods.

I suppose in one very unique way I have been like the longtime resident who hadn't noticed the fireplaces. I have often wondered why a battle for purity rages in my mind. Struggle, repent. Struggle, repent. You know the cycle. At one point it occurred to me that I didn't have obvious or major sin in my life, so why couldn't I be freed from it? I slowly realized I did have sin in my life; maybe it wasn't "big sin" as we like to call it, but it was sin. It was in the television shows and movies I watched. I didn't watch horrible shows, certainly not anything X-rated or even violent. My movies were much nicer than that and presented themselves in pretty packages. They were mostly romance movies with themes of love and compassion. However, beneath the romance, an ugly truth masqueraded, which usually consisted of immorality, adultery, lying, and cheating. The ugliness was hidden and often disguised under admirable themes. Over the years, that's a lot of ugliness and lies that poured into my heart and mind with my own permission. Sadly, movies and television shows are not the only culprits; the ugliness can come from books, magazines, social media, cell phones, and even unhealthy relationships.

Perhaps you are observant and would have noticed the fireplaces right away. Some of them are hidden and disguised, and some stand in wide-open areas. They have been a part of life for a long time and have just blended in with their surroundings. Whether we choose to see them or not, the fireplaces do exist. Just as the fireplaces contribute to the overall character of my community, what we view, read, and listen to contributes to our emotional purity. Unfortunately, while most of us stress physical purity, we give little thought to emotional purity. Yet emotional purity affects everything. It affects what comes out of our mouths, how we view our marriages, and what kinds of women we will become. It affects and shapes our daughters as we model emotional purity to them. God values emotional purity because, ultimately, it is a reflection of what is in our hearts.

I'm wondering how many others have not noticed the fireplaces. As for me, I want to notice …

Chapter 1

Appeal to the Audience

Love the Lord your God with all your heart and with all your soul and with all your mind. This is the first and greatest commandment.

—*Matthew 22:37–38*

Imagine you were given a rare jewel by someone. It was a gift you did not earn or even deserve. The jewel came with simple instructions, to guard it carefully. It became your most prized possession. You took great care of it at first because its value was priceless. Its worth far exceeded anything else you owned. But slowly, over time, you became lazy with the care the jewel required. One day the jewel was left out in the rain where the dark skies and pounding rain struck it. The wet and sticky mud covered it. Particles of sand scratched the delicate surface. Rocks fell on it and chipped away its luster. It was stepped on with hard soles of a shoe, which embedded it further into the ground. It was trampled on day after day until it was no longer even visible. The worst part wasn't that the jewel was left in the rain, scratched, or chipped, but that it was forgotten. Completely forgotten were its value, worth, and beauty. The simple instructions to guard it carefully had not been heeded.

Each of us has been given a rare jewel. The Creator has given us each a heart. It has come with simple instructions. Proverbs 4:23 says, "Above all else, guard your heart, for it is the wellspring of life." The heart is the very essence of who we are. It is the reason we cry with a friend or hurt with her through a loss. We feel the weight of a situation deeply and respond with joy, pain, grief, or anger. You may be a new mom with young kids in diapers or a mom who carpools kids to school and sports activities. Perhaps you are a mom whose children have left for college or who are now married with kids of their own. Maybe you are a newlywed with no children yet. You may still be single or recently back to singlehood. The stage in your life does not matter, because you are a woman. As women, we were created with emotions and minds that are beautiful. God designed us this way—as beautiful creatures that cry at the drop of a hat and love with every ounce of our hearts. Demonstrating emotion is one difference that separates us from our male counterparts, who usually do not feel or demonstrate emotion so profoundly.

Of course, even Jesus felt and outwardly demonstrated emotion. Scripture tells us Jesus wept over the death of a friend and felt the pangs of loneliness. He showed anger when His people were treated unfairly and had compassion on the sick. Emotions are a God-given gift. Without them, we would be callous, cold, and indifferent. We would be like robots unable to feel or respond to anything or anyone. However, with our unique ability to feel emotions so deeply comes an incredible vulnerability, an emotional vulnerability that can take us to dangerous places and lead us into sin.

Do Women Struggle with Pornography?

Most of us have decided on what we believe is pornography. However, if we really understood its definition, we would realize it is far broader than our understanding. In reality, pornography is anything that entices us in impure ways leading to physical or emotional gratification. Pornography satisfies our physical or emotional appetite in unhealthy, inappropriate, and sinful ways. Most women have larger emotional appetites than physical appetites. Women need and want their emotions satisfied. When their emotional needs are satisfied, this usually arouses their physical appetites. Since the emotions require satisfaction, pornography is not just limited to physical impurity. It also includes emotional impurity, especially for women.

An emotional impurity is anything that arouses and satisfies the emotions through inappropriate means. An emotional impurity can take place in many different forms. It can be as simple as being gratified by viewing romance unfold on television or social media. It can be as involved as living out a fantasy life in our minds. It can even be as complicated as an emotional or physical relationship with another man.

In 2003, *Today's Christian Women* found in a survey that one out of every six women, including Christians, acknowledged struggling with pornography.[1]

According to a 2006 survey by the *Internet Filter Review*, 17 percent of women struggle with a pornography addiction.[2]

Women's Services and Resources reported as follows:

- 13 percent of women confess to accessing pornography at work.
- 70 percent of women keep their cyber activities private.
- Women frequent chat rooms two times more than men.
- Women are far more likely than men to act out their behaviors, such as having multiple partners, casual sex, or affairs.[3]

These statistics are astounding considering pornography is considered a "man's problem." After all, many think women don't generally struggle with sexual addictions. Perhaps women do not struggle to the degree that men do, but women do struggle with emotional impurities.

Since pornography includes emotional impurities, I believe the percentage of females struggling with pornography is far greater than 17 percent for a few reasons. First, this research took place several years ago, and when technology advances, the potential for sin also advances. Second, many women do not believe they are engaging in pornography. They don't believe what they're reading or watching is harmful or wrong.

Let's examine some of these explicit portrayals in more detail and explore why 17 percent may be far below the actual percentage of women struggling with pornography.

Books

Explicit books laced with degrading sexual content sell millions of copies. Their target audience is women. A recent 2012 bestseller was called the "fastest selling novel for adults of all time." Its audience is married women over the age of thirty, and it has become increasingly popular among teenage girls and college women as well. Millions of copies of this sexually explicit novel have been sold in the United States alone. Some have labeled the book "mommy porn." Many of its female readers carefully monitor what their little children view and read while failing to monitor what their own eyes see and read.

Television

Women love to watch reality television shows glamorizing the story of someone's life. They become gripped by someone's life, someone they will most likely never meet. Every week, women also watch television shows overflowing with sexual content. One man dates and kisses twenty-five women. In an effort to find his one true love, he breaks hearts along the way. As the female participants in the show ride this emotional roller coaster, they become resentful, angry, and hurt. Most women would never go on such a quest to find their spouses. They would not want their own children looking for future spouses in this manner, either. Yet it's easy to tune into this drama and watch it unfold week after week. Viewer loyalty is confirmation to Hollywood of what the female audience hungers for.

Social Media

Millions of housewives jump on social media after dropping their kids off at school. They often spend hours communicating with friends they barely know or people they might not know at all. Sometimes, their time is spent viewing or reading inappropriate content. These same housewives, however, can be frustrated when their kids arrive home from school and spend too much time on their electronics instead of investing their time in more productive things. They fail to make the connection between what they are doing and what their children are doing.

In many of their own homes, women spend countless hours on movies, books, and social media. These are far from reality and have the potential to divert us from our marriages and families. When we invest time in these things, they take deep root in our realities, slowly controlling what we think about. We pour time and energy into something that has the ability to lead our hearts astray. Most of us would never do the things we read or watch on television, yet we are completely content to view them or read about them. Most of us are wise enough to avoid participating in such immorality, but we are not wise enough to abstain from the mental or emotional impact of viewing or reading about them.

The reality that unfolds is one of hurt, disappointment, and broken marriages. If Satan cannot get us to take part in evil, his alternative is to saturate our minds with it. Just because we may not participate in such things, we aren't immune to their impact on our emotions and our marriages when we view them or read about them.

An Audience with a Different Appetite

Women view or read this content because of an emotional need—a need to be loved, romanced, and communicated with.

Even Scripture points out our need for love. Ephesians 5:25 says, "Husbands, love your wives, just as Christ loved the church and gave himself up for her." God knew we so desperately needed to be loved; He gave the command to our husbands. But women need not only to be loved; they need to feel the love. If we do not feel loved, we try to meet these emotional needs through inappropriate and often sinful avenues. But we are left unsatisfied, empty, and longing for more. These needs are real and should be met but not through some emotional high offered by the entertainment world. When we feed our emotional appetites with inappropriate things, it is sin. This sin can come from television programs, movies, Internet sites, cell phones, novels, magazines, fantasies, or even inappropriate relationships.

Satan has appealed to the female audience. He knows what our weaknesses are and then entices us. He knows what we need and crave. He has targeted women to try to destroy the family from a different angle. Men have received recognition from the church and assistance in their battle with pornography. Women have stood on the sidelines cheering on their men, and now Satan is attacking us cunningly. We are wired very differently from men, and Satan knows that. He knows our weakness lies not in our sexual appetites but in our emotions and in our minds. When he influences our emotions and minds, they become his playground. While men and women share similar struggles, women are more susceptible to the battle of the mind.

Pornography is not just a man's issue anymore; it has now become our issue as well. If you have ever battled this escape with your emotions, you are not alone. Like pornography for men, a woman's battle with her mind and emotions can easily lead to sin if not properly dealt with. This issue is relatively unaddressed in our culture and our churches. Physical purity is stressed, while emotional purity has taken the back seat. One reason this may not be addressed is that women feel shame, guilt, and fear of what others will think. Since we are wired the same way, we share similar struggles, but we are not excused from the evil in our hearts and minds. The sins of men often seem more visible, but the secret sins of women are just as wicked. Men's sins are often physical, and women's sins are often emotional.

Emotional purity is just as important as physical purity. Emotional purity affects everything. The eye is the outlet through which everything is allowed into our minds. It is the gatekeeper. It determines our thought lives, how we view our marriages, and what kinds of women we will become. It affects every part of our beings. Luke 11:34 says, "Your eye is the lamp of your body. When your eyes are healthy, your whole body also is full of light. But when they are unhealthy, your body is also full of darkness." Sin starts in our minds; we do something sinful because we thought about it first. One way we introduce sinful thoughts is when we view, read, or listen to inappropriate things. We do not need outside sources to have sinful thoughts. We are completely sinful on our own. But allowing immorality or emotional impurity from the world to enter our minds does not help our sinful nature.

It is time for women to recognize and stop dancing around these issues. We need to stop pretending everything is fine when it is not. Women have emotional impurities. We need to own up to this struggle and take responsibility for it. We need to let the Holy Spirit stir up conviction in our lives and speak out against the sins that have crept into our churches and homes.

Satan wants us to live in secrecy and shame; paralyzed and alone. There is great victory in exposing darkness to light. Satan hates godly women, and he hates our marriages. We must open our eyes and recognize the bait he is using to lure us into destruction. We must be women who guard our hearts, because the Enemy is waging war against us. Unless we stand with bold conviction and opposition, sin will continue having its way with us, eventually mastering us.

Without emotional purity, we will never become the women Christ desires us to become. Once we expose and repent of our sin, we can become the beautiful women God intended us to be inside and out. Matthew 22:37 says, "Love the Lord your God with all your heart, with all your soul, and with all your mind. This is the first and greatest commandment." Loving God with our hearts and souls seems much easier than loving Him with our minds, but the truth is that all three are connected. When we see where our minds are, we also see where are hearts are. *It is time to repent and reclaim our hearts and minds for Christ.* It is not my place to say if you are into pornography. Only God knows your heart. Be honest with yourself about one question. Are the things you watch and read acceptable and pleasing before a holy God?

Chapter 2

Chick Flicks

I will conduct the affairs of my house with a blameless heart. I will not look with approval on anything that is vile. I hate what faithless people do; I will have no part in it. The perverse of heart shall be far from me; I will have nothing to do with what is evil.

—Psalm 101:3–4

Is there a difference between a woman watching a romantic movie and a man staring at a picture of a naked woman? Many of you are probably thinking, "A man looking at a naked woman is far worse. It's pornography." How about when a woman watching a romantic movie starts to feel emotionally stimulated by the onscreen romance? She feels satisfied by the emotional high the movie offers. Or perhaps she starts fantasizing about a relationship with a man, real or fictitious. It may lead to a physical relationship in her fantasy, or it may stay purely emotional.

How about a woman who is involved in an "innocent" texting relationship with a married man? She finds the texting conversation more appealing than conversations with her own husband and looks forward to them each day. She secretly wishes her husband was more like this man. Perhaps then, she wouldn't be lonely anymore. How about a woman who is reading a novel about an affair down to the most intimate, descriptive detail? She hangs onto every part. She replays the scenes to the point that she cannot get them out of her mind.

So now let me ask you again, is there a difference between a woman watching a romantic movie and a man looking at a picture of a naked woman? If it leads to sin, then one is no different from the other. Both lead the heart astray. The only difference is the technique used to appeal to the audience. For men, it is a physical and sexual attraction. For women, it is a romantic and emotional connection.

Emotional v. Emotional Impurity

We already discussed that feeling emotion is normal and is a gift given to us by the Creator. If emotions are normal, how do we know when we are in sin and not just experiencing normal feelings? It boils down to a question of satisfaction and gratification. Welling up with tears when we watch a movie because we are touched by the display of compassion, tenderness, or romance is a normal emotional reaction. It is when we start to desire or feel the emotion for ourselves—instead of merely reacting to it—that such emotion can become sin. The difference is that the first, merely reacting, is feeling emotional, while the second, internalizing the emotion, satisfies a deep emotional need in our own hearts. This is magnified when the things that satisfy us are void in our own relationships and marriages.

If watching a romantic movie satisfies us so we do not need romance from our own husbands, we have crossed over from feeling emotion to being satisfied by the emotion. Remember, an emotional impurity is anything that arouses and satisfies the emotions through inappropriate means. It is an extremely fine line, one that we as women can easily cross. Other lines are much clearer, such as watching adultery unfold or reading about every little detail of a sizzling affair. Even if we feel these do not provide emotional satisfaction, immersing ourselves in them is not acceptable because we are being entertained by immorality.

I do believe women struggle with pornography, perhaps not physically but emotionally. We may not call it pornography, but if it satisfies an emotional desire leading to gratification, then it is pornography. Some of us dabble in it with certain movies and books. Others have both feet fully immersed through inappropriate texting relationships or affairs. Please don't misunderstand me. I am not saying every love story, every social media connection, or every texting situation is wrong. However, if these things lead you to commit sin, tolerate sin, or consume your mind with sin, then they are wrong. Since we would never tolerate pornography from our husbands or our sons, we should not be willing to tolerate our own sinful compromises in these areas.

We Have Been Deceived

Hollywood is well aware of what appeals to each of the sexes, and writers, producers, and directors know full well what will entertain women. They know what women want and what they will spend their time and money watching. The sad part is many of us have confirmed this to them because we watch their shows. We have catered and contributed to this mentality. They have created a host of shows and movies targeting women and our desire for romance. Many shows, including soap operas, reality shows, and movies, have been targeted to us. Consider even the name given to women's movies. "Chick Flicks" are precisely that—movies women love to watch. Hollywood knows these movies entertain and captivate women. Women are lured by these movies' emotional appeal.

The approach to lure women is much more deceptive than the approach to deceive men. This lure leads back to the garden of Eden. Consider how Eve was deceived with just a slight twist Satan put on God's words. Satan knew Eve's vulnerability and used it to take advantage of her. We are just as easily deceived by tolerating certain media with excuses, such as "it's not as bad as some movies," "there's nothing else to watch," "it's not pornography," or "since my husband isn't romantic with me, it's okay." With a slight twist, we justify sin in our lives. Satan knows what we need and long for and tries to convince us he has the solution. When a man engages in pornography, most everyone would say it is wrong. But when women watch movies and read books all in the name of romance or a good love story, few think twice about it. No one addresses it, confronts it, or even considers it wrong. Perhaps the reason it is not addressed is because it is mostly good mixed in with a little bad. This is why deception is so dangerous; it is mostly truth mixed in with a few lies. But this little bit of lies, no matter how small, taints the whole truth. Adding just one drop of red food coloring to a glass of water will still turn the water pink. It may still taste and look like water, but the red dye is mixed throughout the contents of the glass.

Deception is destruction at its best. It is the Enemy's plan to destroy us from the inside out. Deception is usually delivered slowly over time until the whole vessel is destroyed. With adultery, most women don't just jump into bed with another man. They are slowly lured in. It is a gradual, subtle, and methodical process. It might start out as a conversation or texting relationship that slowly builds with intensity over time. Subtle change is much less noticeable than instant change. It is the tactic of the Enemy who is sneaky, cunning, and deceptive.

If those in Hollywood and the media know how to appeal to us as women, spending millions making movies and using technology to captivate our emotional nature, we should be as well equipped to guard our minds. Unfortunately, most of us are like untrained and unarmed soldiers heading in for the battle of our lives—our marriages. Fighting for our marriages is a daily battle regardless of our circumstances. We easily succumb to the Enemy's tactics when we willingly choose to listen, watch, and read about his schemes. We strip ourselves of any weapons and lie defenseless against him. If we examine our lives closely, we will see the path we chose is full of deception and is nothing but a web of lies. We absorb thoughts, feelings, and images into our fragile and vulnerable minds, and we feel defeated time and time again. It's similar to opening a faucet of water and failing to shut it tightly, so it just drips. Sometimes we open the faucet and fail to shut it off at all, so it runs at full speed. Whether it drips or runs, we don't realize it until everything around us is soaked and ruined. Sometimes that doesn't even catch our attention, so it takes practically drowning to force us to stop and think there may actually be a problem. We wonder why our marriages are so shaky and we feel so unfulfilled. We wonder why we have lost the love for our husbands and lack any communication with them. We may even be entertaining the idea of an affair or divorce for the first time. Yet we are the ones who opened the faucet. We are the ones who failed to turn it off at the first warning signal. We are the ones who failed to install boundaries.

Our Emotional Lives Matter to God

As women, we often escape into our private worlds of emotion and romance. Since actions and speech are visible, we tend to think our thought life remains unseen. Consider, however, the following Scriptures:

- "The Lord saw how great the wickedness of the human race had become on the earth, and that every inclination of the *thoughts* of the human heart was only evil all the time" (Genesis 6:5, emphasis added).
- "You have searched me and you know me. You know when I sit and when I rise, you perceive my *thoughts* from afar" (Psalm 139:1–2, emphasis added).
- "Knowing their *thoughts* Jesus said, why do you entertain evil *thoughts* in your hearts?" (Matthew 9:4, emphasis added).
- "Jesus knew their *thoughts* and said to them, 'Every kingdom divided against itself will be ruined, and every city or household divided against itself will not stand'" (Matthew 12:25, emphasis added).
- "Jesus knowing their *thoughts*, took the little child and had him stand beside Him" (Luke 9:47, emphasis added).

It is apparent from Scripture that God clearly knows our thought life. Nothing is unseen by Him. Jeremiah 23:24 says, "Who can

Irene Sposato

hide in secret places that I cannot see them, declares the Lord.
Do I not fill heaven and earth, declares the Lord." We cannot
run or hide. Jonah could not run from God when he was asked
to go to Nineveh. Isaiah 29:15 says, "Woe to those who go to
great depths to hide their plans from the Lord, who do their
work in darkness and think, who sees us? Who will know?"
The Creator who formed us knows every detail about us, down
to the number of hairs on our heads, and He also knows our
motives, thoughts, and our hearts. Nothing is hidden from Him.

A great illustration of how much our hearts matter to God is
when He sent Samuel to Bethlehem to anoint the future king
of Israel. Samuel was at the house of Jesse, and seven of Jesse's
sons passed before him. Each time he thought, "Surely this
is God's anointed." When God said no to each son, Samuel
began to question if there were any more sons left. Finally,
when David was brought before him, Samuel knew this was
to be the next king. The Bible says, "But the Lord said to
Samuel, do not consider his appearance or his height, for I have
rejected him. The Lord does not look at the things people look
at. People look at the outward appearance, but the Lord looks
at the heart" (1 Samuel 16:7). Our human nature formulates
opinions and judgments based on appearance, but God looks
straight at the heart. In fact, nothing matters more to Him than
the condition of our hearts. If He sees our hearts, He knows
our thoughts, because the heart and the mind are connected. It
matters to God what we think about and where we spend our
thought lives. It matters to Him what we watch and what we
read. Our emotional lives matter to God. It matters because it
ultimately affects our lives and spills into our marriages.

Chapter 3

In Our Hearts, in Our Minds, and in Our Marriages

Therefore, since we have these promises, dear friends, let us purify ourselves from everything that contaminates body and spirit, perfecting holiness out of reverence for God.
—2 Corinthians 7:1

Physically, the heart and the brain are two separate organs in the human body. However, spiritually, the heart and the mind are the same and will be used interchangeably for the remainder of the book. We do not store thoughts, feelings, or emotions in our hearts, but in our minds. We make decisions based on reasoning from our minds. We are told to make decisions with our minds, not our hearts, because feelings can lead us astray. Our minds, however, can control our emotions and our feelings.

In the last chapter we reviewed that Jesus knows what people are thinking. He sees straight through to the heart and knows our very thoughts. Now let's examine what Jesus said about the condition of our hearts and how they affect other areas of our lives:

- "Knowing their thoughts Jesus said, why do you entertain evil thoughts in your hearts?" (Matthew 9:4).
- "For out of the heart come evil thoughts—murder, adultery, sexual immorality, theft, false testimony, slander" (Matthew 15:19).
- "For it is from within, out of a person's heart, that evil thoughts come—sexual immorality, theft, murder, adultery, greed, malice, deceit, lewdness, envy, slander, arrogance and folly. All of these evils come from inside and make a man unclean" (Mark 7:21–23).

Jesus discussed the evil inclination of the heart and how it makes a person unclean three times. Sin is a heart issue because the heart is desperately wicked. Since we are a sinful people and have sinful natures, we will have sinful thoughts. Jeremiah 17:9 says, "The heart is deceitful above all things and beyond cure. Who can understand it?" Every one of us has sinful thoughts that pop into our minds throughout the day. However, there is a big difference between thinking momentarily about something sinful versus feeding the sinful thought. It is what we do with the sinful thought that matters. Playing out sin in our minds and adding in sexual or emotional content so our own emotions and desires are aroused is sinful. Viewing or reading inappropriate content only feeds the sin, making it much harder to escape.

There is also a difference between sinful thoughts and resting our thought lives consistently on sin. When we choose to constantly feed our minds with impurity, this shapes us and impurity begins to define us. The Bible says, "As a man thinks in his heart, so is he" (NKJV Proverbs 23:7). What we think about is essentially who we are. We cannot take baths in dirty water and expect to come out clean. We will smell to those around us, soil our own clothes, and leave dirty tracks behind. Our dirty bath water will affect everyone and everything around us. It will leave marks on our marriages and other relationships.

The heart spills into other areas, just like the dirty bath water. Matthew 12:34 says, "The mouth speaks from the overflow of the heart." Since the mouth speaks from the heart, we can conclude what we say comes directly from our thoughts. There is a direct connection between our mouths and our thought lives. When my child speaks unkind or cruel words, I can give him a consequence. But the real root of the problem lies within his heart. His heart needs to be clean in order for his mouth to become clean. In order for his heart to be clean, his thoughts need to be clean. We can clean up our mouths without dealing with the root of the problem, but we have only dealt with it temporarily. Our thoughts are the real problem, since they affect the condition of our hearts. Those thoughts come from sin we have allowed to enter our hearts.

Often we are tempted to think our thought lives remain private. No one will know and no one will find out. But if the mouth spews out what is really in our hearts, then everyone sees the ugliness because it can't help but spill out. Each of us has had moments where we have shocked ourselves because of what we said. We usually say something because we were thinking it first. Whether or not we mean it, it comes out. The ugly words seep into our marriage relationships and can sow seeds of hurt and devastation. They sting and leave marks behind. Even after apologizing, we can never take them back.

The heart can even affect the way we feel. It can lead to thoughts, which can trigger feelings. Feelings can sometimes lead us to make foolish choices and engage in careless behavior. In chapter 1, we learned that women are far more likely to act out their pornography-inspired behavior (affairs, casual sex). This may start with a thought where time and energy were carefully invested. The thought can lead to a feeling and can eventually lead to a behavior. We will examine feelings further in a later chapter. For now, we need to recognize that our thoughts can affect our feelings.

When we get the stomach flu, bacteria enters our stomachs, and our bodies are forced to expel it in some way. Whether up or down, it must come out. It is a toxin that needs to be expelled. Like the toxin in our stomachs, the toxin in our hearts will come out one way or the other. We can only hide or fake it for so long. Eventually, it will seep out. At some point, everyone will see the condition of our hearts. The ugliness is so putrid and wretched that we cannot hide it from God or from others. One part of us affects our whole beings, just as a drop of red dye affects the entire glass of water. Our thought lives are cycles that are reflected in our speech, feelings, and actions.

Consider Joan, who thought she was happy in her marriage. One day, her eyes were opened to something else. Her neighbor Nancy always seemed to be getting new things; really nice things. Nancy's husband traveled the world for business and was always bringing her expensive purses and jewelry. The way Nancy showcased her newest treasures didn't help. Joan always learned about them through social media. At first, Joan was happy for her friend. But slowly, over time, discontentment set in. Joan wondered why her husband didn't bring her gifts when he traveled. She would settle for a small one. Then she began to think she deserved gifts and started to hint about them to her husband. When her husband didn't catch the hints, she became bitter and resentful toward him. The more she entertained the discontentment and bitterness, the deeper its roots went. Soon she had convinced herself that she deserved more than just gifts—she deserved a better husband who could provide her with such luxuries.

As women, we can convince ourselves of pretty much anything. We can convince ourselves we deserve more, or we can convince ourselves we need new husbands. When we consume ourselves with something, it has the power to impact the choices we make in our marriages. When we spend time on things other than the truth of God's Word, they can control us and influence how we live our lives. Those thoughts will shape us, define us, and make us who we are. They will dictate how we treat our husbands and the value we place on our marriage relationships. If our thoughts have the power to affect us so deeply, we must be careful about where they are invested. Scripture speaks of our hearts following our treasure: "For where your treasure is, there your heart will be also" (Matthew 6:21). Most of us apply this verse to the principle of money. The kinds of things we invest our money in are essentially where our hearts are. This same principle can be applied to other treasures, such as time, energy, and where we invest our thought lives. We invest in things we deem important. Our hearts follow that investment. If we invest in the wrong things, our hearts can be filled with impurity. This impurity can negatively affect our marriages.

Sue loved logging onto her social media website. It was an easy and convenient way to find college roommates and old friends.

It was fun catching up on friends' lives and swapping pictures of their children. When an old boyfriend wanted to connect with her, she gladly accepted. Given their broken engagement over ten years ago, she was all too eager to discover who he had married and what his life was like. Scrolling through his profile and pictures, memories flooded her mind. The brief comments they exchanged led to longer conversations. Reminiscing about the past with her old flame stirred her emotions. Soon, she couldn't escape the feelings she once felt for him. It was as if their love was being rekindled. The more she thought about him, the stronger her feelings became.

According to the *New York Daily News*, in 2009 Facebook was named in one in five divorce cases in the United States.[4] *The Guardian* reported on a 2010 survey conducted by the American Academy of Matrimonial Lawyers, which revealed that four out of five lawyers reported an increase in the number of divorces due to social networking sites.[5] These are alarming statistics for a social media website whose primary purpose is to connect and reconnect family and friends. Despite the statistics, Facebook isn't tearing marriages apart. People are doing that. Like anything else in life, when used incorrectly and without boundaries, social media can be both harmful and destructive. It can lead to feelings and behaviors that destroy marriages.

Our hearts, our minds, and our marriages are all connected. Where we invest our thought lives will affect every part of our lives. The things we invest our thoughts in will affect the condition of our hearts. The condition of our hearts seeps in and affects our marriages.

Fill Your Plate with Vegetables

When Adam and Eve sinned, they brought sin into the world. Psalm 14:3 says, "All have turned away, all have become corrupt; there is no one who does good, not even one." This is uncontrollable. The world is sinful and will continue to be sinful until Christ returns. We cannot change or control the sin that has been brought into this world. What we can control is what we put into our hearts and minds. A doctor will tell us what the risk factors are for certain diseases. Some risk factors, such as age, heredity, or race, cannot be controlled. Other risk factors, such as diet, exercise, smoking, and drinking, can be controlled. The latter are risk factors because of the lifestyles we live. Doctors advise us to control these risk factors to minimize our likelihood of getting certain diseases. If we ignore this medical advice, we are likely to suffer the consequences for our choices.

Likewise, God gives us instruction for protecting our minds. This instruction is designed to minimize problems and sin in our lives. God provides a very clear road map for our thought lives, a map that leads to emotional purity. Philippians 4:7–9 says, "And the peace of God, which transcends all understanding, will guard your hearts and minds in Christ Jesus. Whatever is true, whatever is right, whatever noble, whatever is pure, whatever is lovely, whatever is admirable—if anything is excellent or praiseworthy—think about such things. Whatever you have learned or received or heard from me, or seen in me—put it into practice. And the peace of God will be with you."

Every woman knows the best way to avoid eating the wrong foods is to fill her plate with the right foods. When we fill our

23

plates with salad and vegetables, there isn't room for french fries. When we meditate on the lovely and the admirable, there isn't room for evil and destructive thoughts. When we focus on the truth, lies have a harder time squeezing in. We need to fill our minds with the right thoughts so the wrong thoughts have no room to get in. Scripture tells us that when we meditate on the right thoughts, we will have the peace of God. God's peace transcends because God is stronger and more powerful than even our most consuming thoughts. The key is to submit our thoughts to His ways so His peace can guard our thought lives. We cannot realistically expect peace if we do not follow the guidelines God has given us. We cannot expect healthy bodies if we consume only french fries, and we cannot expect pure thought lives if we consistently saturate our minds with impurity.

Impure and destructive thoughts can be triggered by viewing emotional and physical adultery, premarital sex, homosexuality, lying, cheating, lust, and greed. There is enough evil around us. We do not need to watch the details of these immoral themes unravel on television. While the Bible may not speak about television or other media sources, it is very clear that our thought lives should be holy and pleasing to God.

When our minds are occupied with a false reality, we are vulnerable and may not even recognize the threats that lie before us. Some of us are so saturated in emotional impurity that we are not able to recognize the danger. We give Satan an open invitation for evil and may be desensitized to his presence. Job 1:7 says, "The Lord said to Satan, 'Where have you come from?' Satan answered the Lord, 'From roaming throughout the earth, going back and forth on it.'" Like a hungry lion roaming for food, the Enemy's purpose is to kill, steal, and destroy. The Enemy is no fool and knows what we tolerate in our thought lives. He knows who is weak. He knows who is vulnerable, and he knows who has her guard down. He is at work right now planning to destroy women, marriages, and families. He knows that destroying marriages destroys the very foundation of society. If he has a plan, we must have a plan as well. We cannot afford to just sit by. The emotional impurity that seeps into our thought lives is just like a running faucet that nobody notices. If we are to be the holy women God designed us to be, we must clean up our thought lives and willingly choose what we allow to enter our minds.

Chapter 4

Gray

"This is the covenant I will make with the people of Israel after that time," declared the Lord. "I will put my law in their minds and write it on their hearts. I will be their God and they will be my people."
—*Jeremiah 31:33*

Beautiful Women, Inside and Out

As women, we go to great lengths in the choices we make daily. We carefully choose the outfits we will wear. We can invest hours on the Internet, searching for just the right pair of shoes. We purchase, return, and purchase again. We spend time getting our hair styled and colored. Wanting the right look for our homes, we often arrange and rearrange many times. We read labels at grocery stores because we want the best for our families. We buy special foods and avoid certain foods based on research. We sign up for spin and dance classes. We run, train, and set lofty goals. We carefully read the tags for laundering the cute sweaters we purchase. Most of us are good mothers, cautiously overseeing what our children watch, hear, and read. However, we often give very little thought to some of the impurities we allow into our own minds. We protect our children but often fail to safeguard ourselves. There is nothing wrong with wanting our wardrobe, hair, bodies, and homes to look beautiful. However, if we do not apply the same level of excellence to our emotional purity, we are missing the mark Christ has called us to.

We sometimes watch movies portraying an early theme of adultery. Despite this, we continue watching. We purchase best-selling novels only to discover they contain explicit sexual content. Yet, we continue reading. While we commit to high levels of excellence in certain areas of our lives, our emotional purity tends to hang somewhere in the middle between evil and excellence. When it comes to our emotional purity, we tend to be halfway holy. Half-hearted attempts at emotional purity are really no attempts at holiness at all. Holiness is the antithesis of evil. Half-hearted attempts are not even close.

Suppose you wanted your living room painted a new color to complement the pillows you found on sale over the weekend. After considering countless possibilities, you finally settle on a bold red color. You hire a painter and hand him the "cayenne pepper" paint chip. You leave for the day and return with excitement to see the change. Walking through the door, you can smell the fresh paint. Your feet come to a complete halt when you set your eyes on the finished work. You stare in disbelief at pink walls. This was not what you were expecting. The painter notices the look of despair on your face and immediately starts to explain. Although you wanted cayenne pepper, he felt "strawberry lemonade" suited you much better. After years of experience, he feels he knows his clients' tastes better than they do, which leads him to intervene when they choose the wrong color. He decided to move forward with the strawberry lemonade color, trusting you would be in agreement. At this point, you walk over to the sofa and pull out the new pillows underneath the drop cloth. You explain that they were the inspiration for the cayenne pepper color. The painter is speechless because he thought he was right. If only he had known about the pillows beforehand.

We are often like the painter. We take matters into our own hands, thinking we know ourselves better than our Designer. We think we know better because we do not understand the design God has in mind for us. God is our Designer and has masterfully planned and orchestrated our lives and our minds for holiness. He knows exactly what will coordinate best with our emotions and thought lives. He knows what things will benefit and what things will damage our minds. Many of us do not know the plan of the Designer because we have not taken the time to consult Him. We take matters into our own hands and choose colors that are incompatible with those of the Designer. When we invest in things that compromise our emotional purity, we are straying from the plan the Designer has chosen for us. In these moments, we are no better than lukewarm for Christ.

Lukewarm

In Revelation, John writes letters to seven churches. Listen to what he says about the church in Laodicea in Revelation 3:15–16: "I know your deeds, that you are neither cold nor hot. I wish you were either one or the other! So, because you are lukewarm—neither hot nor cold—I am about to spit you out of my mouth." Of the seven churches John addresses, Laodicea is the worst offender because its members were lukewarm. Lukewarm is sitting on the fence; it is being in the middle and never taking a stand for anything. This church was rebuked for being neither hot nor cold. John says it would be better to be cold than lukewarm. It is similar to a water bottle left in a car on a hot day. The water is tasteless and offers no refreshment. We usually prefer hot drinks or cold drinks, not lukewarm drinks.

Christ is so sickened by lukewarm lives that He spits them out of His mouth. He detests them because He is a holy God. The frightening part of all of this is that the church may be the biggest culprit. The church is full of lukewarm people. The worst place to be lukewarm is in our relationship with Christ, because everything in our individual lives hinges on this key relationship.

Like anything in life, we are usually for or against something. We must take this same approach with our emotional purity. Our thought lives will either please or not please God. There is no middle ground. There is no halfway holiness. Isaiah prophesied about it, and Jesus reminded us of his words in Matthew 15:7–9: "You hypocrites! Isaiah was right when he prophesied about you: These people honor me with their lips, but their hearts are far from me. They worship me in vain; their teachings are merely human rules." The media and relationships in our lives will either point us toward holiness or unholiness. They will fill our minds with destructive thoughts or pure and lovely thoughts. If Christ is truly our Lord, what our eyes see, what our ears listen to, and the thoughts we entertain should be centered on holiness.

Christ did not come, suffer, and die for us to sit on the fence. He did not come so we could give half of our hearts to Him. He wants lives fully committed to Him, which includes minds fully committed to Him. If we are in the middle, then we have one foot in holiness and the other foot in evil. The prophet Elijah dealt with this when the nation of Israel had become polluted with idol worship under King Ahab. He said to Ahab in 2 Kings 18:21, "How long will you waiver between two opinions? If the Lord is God, follow him; but if Baal is god, follow him." We need to choose whom we will serve. Sadly, many of us have already chosen which side we are on by the choices we have made on a daily basis.

Holiness Required, Even in Our Minds

In the Old Testament, God resided with the people, and He established many rules about the specifications, details, and handling of the ark of the covenant. The priests had rules regarding their facial hair, clothes, and even the kinds of wives they could marry (Leviticus 21). This was to show the separation between the people and a holy God. He was so holy He could not tolerate an offense, and the offender had to be put to death in most cases. Earlier in Leviticus we read, "You must not live according to the customs of nations I am going to drive out before you. Because they did all these things, I abhorred them… You are to be holy because I, the Lord, am holy and I have set you apart from the nations to be my own" (Leviticus 20:23, 26). God made it very clear that His people are a holy people, and He called them to live differently from the nations around them.

In the New Testament, Jesus abolished the law, but He set the standard even higher. He made known that it is our motives and intent that are His concern. Jesus emphasized that sin is not merely a physical act, but it is also an issue of the heart. If a woman hates her neighbor in her heart, then she has murdered. If a woman lusts after a friend's husband in her heart, then she has committed adultery. Things we fill our minds with matter to God. Jesus said, "Love the Lord your God with all your heart, with all your strength and with all your mind." We must do a better job of protecting our hearts and our minds.

Chapter 5

Holy Women: Part 1

And a highway will be there; it will be called the Way of Holiness; it will be for those who walk on that way. The unclean will not journey on it, wicked fools will not go about on it.

—Isaiah 35:8

If we are being entertained by a sexually explicit reading or television show, we are in sin. If we are engaging in inappropriate texting, we are in sin. In 2 Timothy 3:6 Paul wrote, "They are the kind who worm their way into homes and gain control over gullible women, who are loaded down with sins and are swayed by all kind of evil desires, always learning but never able to come to a knowledge of the truth." Paul wrote this letter because Ephesus had a societal problem with false teachers. These false teachers found their way into the church through certain women who were gullible, weighed down with sin, and full of evil desires. These women never understood the truth. They were always on the receiving end and never on the giving end. The false teachers took advantage of them because the women were entangled in sin. The kinds of things women sought after back then probably weren't much different from today. One may have envied another woman's toga, sandals, or marriage. Someone else probably had her eye on her neighbor's husband, and another was most likely unfaithful in her marriage. The times may have been different, but women are women, and their battles have been the same. Scripture is full of stories of adulterous women. Since most women commit adultery for emotional reasons, emotional sins had to have been prevalent. Little has changed from biblical times to our modern day. The main difference is Satan has used technology and media as the door to invade our hearts and minds. He has used them to creep into our churches, our homes, and our marriages.

Since God is holy, He has called us to be holy women whose lives are set apart from the rest of the world. He calls us to operate based on His truth and not on our feelings. This is not a suggestion, recommendation, or guideline. It is a command. It is not the way of the world. It isn't popular. However, it is a life we must choose if we know Christ. If we are to be holy women, holiness must be an attribute of our lives and our minds. We will not glorify God without having holiness in our minds.

A Holy Woman's Entertainment Window Is Small and Narrow

We are designed to be holy first. Everything else in life is to fit within the parameters of holiness. Whatever we are, mother, wife, friend, nurse, or teacher, we are first called to be holy. Holiness must be the attribute for every area of life. Holiness is the very nature of God. The Bible says, "Be holy because I am Holy" (1 Peter 1:15). It is who God is and what makes Him God. It must be our standard as well, since we are called to be like Him. Holiness is the Designer's plan for us. Far too many of us quickly drift away from this standard for our thought lives. When we drift away from this standard, we compromise. Most of our compromise is on things we think are small. However, these small things quickly add up and eventually define who we are. One unwholesome movie may not seem like a big deal, but a series of such movies corrodes our thinking.

Lisa is hooked on her television series. It's safe to say she is addicted. Her schedule as a nightshift nurse allows her to watch her shows when they are on during the day. There are two particular shows she watches. They are on back to back, making her addiction very convenient. She has even given up lunch dates with girlfriends because her shows are on. When her job situation changes, requiring a move to the day shift, she starts recording them. She now comes home from work and watches while her kids play in the background. She doesn't really know why she's so interested. It seems to be the same storyline over and over again—adulterous affairs mixed in with scandal. Someone cheats on his wife with his cousin's girlfriend only to find out that his wife is pregnant by his best friend or something like that. There is plenty of drama, lying, cheating, and sneaking around. Lisa, like many of us, has plenty of other responsibilities, and she often wonders if she is wasting time. She finds herself playing out the scenarios in her mind when she is with her own family. She counts down the hours until her kids go to bed so she can continue watching.

Regularly watching shows like this will affect how we treat our husbands, our kids, and others. We must not be deceived into thinking these hints of impurity are harmless and will stay nicely tucked in our minds. They will shape the way we think, and if they shape the way we think, they will shape the kind of women we become. *We need to be women who look at the entertainment world through God's standard of holiness.* We cannot let the entertainment world define what is acceptable. We shouldn't watch a particular movie when it doesn't fit through the window of holiness. We will likely become frustrated because most things won't fit through this window. We should not expect most movies, shows, books, or Internet sites to fit. Even Jesus said in Matthew 7:14, "But small is the gate and narrow the road that leads to life, and only a few find it." Holiness is a tight squeeze, not a five-lane highway. The window for holiness is small, and few things fit through it in this world. Holiness is a small gap between two rocks. It is hard and difficult to squeeze through. It is often a struggle and requires work, time, and effort. We should not be surprised when we feel left out or awkward. It is normal to feel as if we don't belong. It is normal when there are very few people who live life as we do. We need to share this truth with our children so they can understand why we say no to certain activities or play dates. God said this earth and this life are not our homes because we are not citizens of this world. We are a people set apart. God called us to be different: "But you are a chosen people, a royal priesthood, a holy nation, God's special possession, that you may declare the praises of him who called you out of darkness into his wonderful light" (1 Peter 2:9).

If we adopt the entertainment values of this world, we need to ask ourselves some hard questions about whether these meet God's standard of holiness. Holiness is often defined by the world as small, tight, and rigid. The world gasps and feels confined by its narrow boundaries. However, it is because of these very narrow boundaries that we feel safety and security.

When we live within the boundaries of holiness, we are held close and firm by our Savior, and our footing is fixed and secure. When we enter through the five-lane highway of the world, we have no walls and no boundaries. We are deceived into believing the five-lane highway represents freedom, but it is just the opposite. It's similar to baby toys with different shapes that each fit through only one opening. When we have the right opening with the right shape turned just the right way, they fit. We can certainly make a shape fit into an opening it wasn't designed for but not without bending or cracking the walls. We can force the shape in, but we end up with damage. The condition of our thought lives may be wild and free. Eventually, insecurities and troubles come. We have nothing to lean on because we removed and damaged all the walls. We end up with damage because we forced something that didn't fit through God's standard of holiness. We cry out to God and wonder where He is, but we chose not to live within His boundaries. We chose the path without the walls. When we submit our thought lives to God's standard of holiness, God gives us the very thing we desire most: His security.

A Holy Woman Feeds More Than She Consumes

Babies are completely dependent on someone else to meet their every need. They need to be fed, changed, bathed, and dressed. Paul says some believers are like spiritual babies in their faith. Ephesians 4:13–14 says, "Until we all reach unity in the faith and in the knowledge of the Son of God and become mature, attaining to the whole measure of fullness of Christ. Then we will no longer be infants, tossed back and forth by the waves, and blown here and there by every wind of teaching and by the cunning and craftiness of people in their deceitful scheming." Spiritual babies are often too young to know what they stand for or what they believe. They are often blown every direction by the wind. They are easily captivated by others and have difficulty standing on their own two feet. We need to do a real-life assessment here and ask ourselves, "Are we babies in our faith, or are we mature, holy women of Christ?" If you are a new believer, your infancy in the faith is understandable for now, because you are still learning and growing. However, if you have remained a spiritual baby for years, then it is time to make a change.

There is a difference between needing encouragement and spiritual dependency. Everyone needs friends for support, wisdom, and occasionally help getting back on one's feet. Needing someone to constantly hold our hands and relying on someone to always lift us to our feet is spiritual dependency. We tend to get it backwards. We are often more dependent on others and less dependent on Jesus. The problem with depending solely on others is it trains us to go to them first and not to the Word of God. Eventually, they will be unable or unwilling to meet our need. The bigger problem is relying solely on someone else and not on Jesus. This spiritual handholding cannot last forever. The only hand we should be constantly holding is that of Jesus. *We need to be women who are spiritually dependent on Jesus and not on anyone or anything else.* Through the years, we should strive and expect to grow spiritually just as we do in our professions or other areas of our lives. Our dependency on Jesus should increase year by year. Everything in life grows and matures. If they didn't, most of us would ask questions, demand answers, and seek resolutions. We wouldn't stop until we had all the answers.

If our toddlers weren't walking by their second birthday, we would seek answers from experts regardless of the cost. We should not be satisfied to remain in the same place spiritually either. Our thought lives need to grow. For our thought lives to grow, we cannot flood them with the impurities of the world. Let's ask ourselves the hard questions and be willing to pay the price. Our spiritual and emotional health are worth it. Babies eventually grow up, and spiritual babies should as well.

Babies are also very immature in actions and in thoughts. They have very self-centered natures. They think the world revolves around them, and whatever satisfies them is best. Babies scream loudly to get their needs met. Spiritual babies are self-centered as well; they can't serve or minister to anyone else because all they think about is themselves. We all have encountered a woman who is a spiritual baby: she only talks about herself. You ask the questions, and she talks and talks about herself and her problems. She never asks you a single question. She overlooks asking how you are because she is so consumed with herself. She can't be interested in you because she only desires what makes her feel good. She is wrapped up in herself because she is spiritually immature. If we lack interest in other people and are unable to minister to them, something is wrong, and we need to start investigating. Is there sin in our lives? Are we reading Scripture daily? How is our prayer life? *We need to be women whose lives are centered on others and not just ourselves.* God calls us to be women who are genuinely interested in the lives of others. God desires for us to give and not just take.

When sin is present in our lives, we tend to be very self-centered. Ephesians 4:17–19 says, "So I tell you this, and insist on it in the Lord, that you must no longer live as the Gentiles do, in the futility of their thinking. They are darkened in their understanding and separated from the life of God because of the ignorance that is in them due to the hardening of their hearts. Having lost all sensitivity, they have given themselves over to sensuality so as to indulge in every kind of impurity, and they are full of greed." Sexual or emotional impurity and greed go hand in hand. We become greedy to satisfy our lust. Sin can cause us to go to extreme measures even at the cost of hiding it from our friends and our husbands. This is why people who are stuck in sin separate themselves from their loved ones. Sin separates. It separates us from God and from the people we love. It desensitizes us to anyone else's needs because we are so consumed with our own sin. Sometimes there are other reasons people are wrapped up in themselves. Pain or tragedy could be the explanation, but most often it is because they are so deeply entrenched in their own sin that they can't see beyond themselves.

Emotional sin will also isolate us. Sin brings us to a place of loneliness and isolation. We want to be by ourselves to continue to live in sin, especially if the sin is an addiction. But mainly we are isolated because sin cannot tolerate the light and will naturally repel those "in the light." Darkness and light have nothing in common. When we make poor choices, we don't want to hang out with our Christian girlfriends for fear of being exposed. Being around other Christians heaps guilt on us. We would rather choose women whose lifestyles reflect ours. This makes living in sin easier for us. We want people around us who affirm us and make us feel good. This mindset can bring isolation and make us more vulnerable to the Enemy. Then Satan has us exactly where he wants us: alone. Just as the lost sheep is more prone to predators, so is a Christian living an isolated life. Even if you are a woman who prefers to be by herself, you are not exempt from this. Any isolation is the perfect prey for the Enemy. Christ didn't call us to live isolated lives, and if you do not have any Christian girlfriends, you need to get a few. You are living in danger when you are alone. You don't need many, but pray for God to bring you at least one godly girlfriend to constantly point you to Christ.

Christ calls us to be women who love and care for others as much as we care for ourselves. This is what it means to "love thy neighbor as thyself." We are to be women who give more than we take and serve more than we are served.

A Holy Woman Accepts Romance Only from Within Her Marriage

When we choose to live for Christ, we are called to change our actions and speech. It is necessary and wonderful to change these things, but it is not enough. Our minds must change as well. Ephesians 4:20–24 says, "That, however, is not the way of life you learned when you heard about Christ and were taught in him in accordance with the truth that is in Jesus. You were taught, with regard to your former way of life, to put off your old self, which is being corrupted by its deceitful desires; to be made new in the attitude of your minds; and to put on the new self, created to be like God in true righteousness and holiness."

Amy is a good mother who wakes up at the crack of dawn, packs lunches, and then drives her crew to school every morning. She rushes home and turns on her television. She surfs the guide for the reality shows she has recorded. She used to watch only a select few, but lately her list has grown. She settles for one and begins watching and seeing the beautiful homes, luxury cars, and expensive vacations. The wife in the reality show appears to have it all together. The husband pops in during the day to surprise her with lunch. He lovingly gazes into her eyes and listens attentively as she shares details about her day. Amy wonders if her life would be "more together" as well if her husband popped home during the day. She feels emotionally satisfied, especially since communication is lacking in her own marriage. She consoles herself, knowing she has an avenue to turn to since her husband doesn't satisfy her need for communication.

We can tolerate emotional impurity when entertainment stirs an emotional response of connection and romance. As women, we generally long for the emotional rather than the sexual connection. We are feeding the flesh to satisfy a longing or desire. We need to offer the deepest longings of our hearts to God: the secret pains and yearnings no one may know about. The cries of our hearts cause us to ache, and they never seem to go away, no matter how hard we try. We need to offer them to God, or else we will attempt to fill them ourselves.

Kate is struggling in her marriage. She and her husband may live in the same house, but their lives are like two ships passing in the night. They hardly communicate except when necessary. Kate may not have a relationship with her husband, but she does have a relationship. It is with a man named Steve. He is handsome, smart, and funny. He is kind and always has time for her. He fulfills the needs that her husband doesn't. The good news is she will never be discovered because no one knows Steve. The bad news is he is very real and lives in her fantasies.

When I was a teenager, my friends and I shared a joke together. We used the word "rotic" because it was the word *romantic* without the "man" in it. It was funny back when I was a young girl, but many married women still operate in this mindset. They escape into a fictitious world or into the arms of another man. Romance is such a driving force for women that we must be careful of its source. Accepting it from anyone or anything except our husbands is wrong. Your husband should be the only "man" in your physical and emotional romance. Even if we aren't getting what we desire, we don't suddenly gain the right to seek it from media or fantasy lives. *We need to be women who turn to our husbands for romance.* It can even captivate single women who are longing for husbands. Do not be misled into thinking you can escape into your fantasy because you are single. The problem arises when you get married and struggle to turn from your fantasy. It is not just a switch you can turn on and off. Marriage has enough concerns of its own. Bringing your fantasy into it will only complicate matters.

A Holy Woman Does Not Tolerate a Hint of Impurity in Her Mind

According to *Merriam-Webster's Dictionary*, a *hint* means "a slight indication of something, a very small amount."[6] Recipes often call for a pinch of this and a pinch of that. The pinch seems so insignificant at the moment. However, when the meal is done, the pinch lends to the overall flavor of the entire dish. A little bit affects a whole thing. The same is true for our minds. Ephesians 5:3–4 says, "But among you there must not be even a hint of sexual immorality, or of any kind of impurity, or of greed, because these are improper for God's holy people. Nor should there be obscenity, foolish talk or course joking, which are out of place, but rather thanksgiving." The easiest place for women to have hints, especially of emotional impurity, is in our minds. But even a hint is too much, because it is sin. A little bit of sin affects every area of our lives.

When my daughter was young, there was a show she really liked to watch on television. Every day at the same time, I would turn it on for her. I looked forward to this time my toddler was occupied because I also had a newborn. This gave me a chance to catch up on some things around the house. Over time, I began to observe a behavior in my daughter that I didn't like. It was the way she spoke to people. She would speak in baby talk using only one word at a time. Quickly my husband and I discovered she was learning it from this particular show. I was frustrated because the show was cute, clean, and entertaining. I had to decide whether the show was worth letting her watch.

Some of us view entertainment with much bigger hints. Those hints usually come in some form of sexual or emotional impurity. Sometimes the impurity is so slight we don't give much thought to it. We have been with the hints so long that they don't bother us anymore; they have just become part of our lives. Anytime we tolerate sin, even by watching it, we slowly become accustomed to it. We develop immunity so that it no longer affects us as it once did. It becomes the "new normal" that we can justify. Slowly, we justify more and more. That's why many of us who watch movies with adulterous themes are no longer bothered by them. In many cases, we have been watching them far too long. We may turn on a show and actually expect it to have adultery. It becomes normal. But it isn't normal, and we need to stop believing the lie. Even if we still believe adultery is wrong, we become tolerant of it. It doesn't grieve us as it once did. Watching a sin unfold over and over again, even if it is not our own sin, desensitizes us until we become numb. Becoming numb to a sin is dangerous, because we are so desensitized that we lack any urgency to run from it. We may not recognize it as evil anymore. We have become so accustomed to it that it becomes a normal expectation of life.

A romance movie with the portrayal of adultery is sexual immorality. The entire movie is compromised because of the underlying theme. Many times we have said, "There's only one bad scene in it," but how many bad scenes does it take before we draw the line and turn the channel? One should be bad enough. We treat sin as if it has some maximum cap. However, sin does not have boundaries beyond which it really qualifies as sin. In God's eyes, ten sins are the same as one. One sin is enough for God. Consider how many swear words it would take on television to turn the channel for your child. For most of us, it wouldn't take ten words.

Tolerating hints of emotional sin will make us vulnerable to other sins. Sin breeds sin. Sin doesn't shrink or disappear; it doesn't even stay the same. It has the potential to grow from a small problem to a huge addiction if given enough time and energy. Sin will take us further than we wanted to go, cost us more than we wanted to pay, and keep us longer than we intended to stay. Romans 6:12–13 says, "Therefore do not let sin reign in your mortal body so that you obey its evil desires. Do not offer any part of yourself to sin as an instrument of wickedness, but rather offer yourselves to God as those who have been brought from death to life; and offer every part of yourself to him as an instrument of righteousness." Scripture is clear that when sin is present, it will have its way with us. It is a dangerous and destructive path similar to standing in the middle of a highway with a semi-truck headed for us. Eventually it will hit us. It may not hit us the first day or even the first week, but one day we will be hit. Sin is like a spider's web. It entangles and is nearly impossible to escape. The more we try to wiggle ourselves out, the more entangled we become. When we are stuck in one sin, it opens us up to a host of other sins with far greater consequences. *We need to be women who do not tolerate hints of impurity.*

Chapter 6

Holy Women: Part 2

Those who live according to the flesh have their minds set on what the flesh desires, but those who live in accordance with the Spirit have their minds set on what the Spirit desires. The mind governed by the flesh is death; but the mind governed by the Spirit is life and peace. The mind governed by the flesh is hostile to God; it does not submit to God's law, nor can it do so. Those who are in the realm of the flesh cannot please God.
—Romans 8:5–8

A Holy Woman Is Content with What God Has Given Her

Tolerating sin in our minds will rob us of joy-filled lives and make us discontented. We may become discontented when someone else's reality makes us realize what we do not have in our own marriages. They make us jealous and covet things other than what God has given us. One small seed of discontentment can turn into a raging fire of jealousy. The middle school years that accompany most young girls are filled with jealousy and incredible insecurity. Jealousy can appear when the new girl is prettier or another has a more hip and more expensive backpack. Often as grown women, it seems we are no different from middle school girls. We are jealous when the new mom drives a nicer car or lives in a more upscale neighborhood. We compare the expensive jewelry her husband gave her on Valentine's Day to the box of chocolates we received. We see her tropical vacation on social media and contrast it with the outing we got at a local restaurant for our birthday. We think that our man should be and could be doing the same things for us. We convince ourselves that we also deserve them. We wonder where our husbands were when God was handing out instructions on "how to love your wives." Realizing they were probably out golfing, hunting, or fishing makes us even angrier. Discontentment sets in, which is a prime tactic of the Enemy.

We often believe the lie that someone else "has it made," especially when we catch glimpses of what appears to be a picture-perfect life. We need to realize this is only our perception and not an accurate portrayal of reality. We tend to only see the glamour instead of the real day-to-day real life. We somehow never see the posts from the wife whose husband forgot her birthday or from the couple whose son failed math class. Even the reality shows are beefed up to make them more appealing. They create hype, which only amounts to more drama. We cannot safely assume reality shows are accurate portrayals of anyone's lifestyle. The old saying, "the grass is greener on the other side of the fence," couldn't be more inaccurate. A more accurate spin would be, "the grass is greener where you fertilize it." We make the mistake of staring at lawns in dire need of water when our own lawns are starving for fertilizer.

Beth has been lonely in her marriage for some time. Her husband is always working late at the office or going out with the guys. He never seems to have time for her anymore. The days of flowers or unexpected notes are a thing of the past. She can't even remember the last time the two of them spent any quality time together. Now that the kids are older and don't need her as much, she spends much of her time alone. She felt really alone until a text came from her son's baseball coach one day. Even though it was meant to communicate practice times, Beth took it for much more. She answered him back in appreciation, which led to a compliment and has now turned into a texting relationship. She feels noticed because he pays attention to her, making her feel young and pretty again. There is no physical relationship, so she feels justified; she figures she deserves more than her husband is giving her.

As with Beth, loneliness can easily lead to discontentment. Sometimes we think we have a right to be discontented, especially if it is something we think we deserve. Spiritually, we do not deserve anything. God gives us gifts only due to His great mercy and grace. Ephesians 2:8 says, "For it is by grace you have been saved, through faith—and this is not from yourselves, it is the gift of God—not by works, so no one can boast." We do need certain things in our marriages, but not receiving them does not give us the right to seek them from inappropriate sources. *We need to be women who are content, regardless of the state of our marriages.* Paul says in Philippians 4:12, "I have learned the secret of being content in any and every situation, whether well fed or hungry, whether living in plenty or want. I can do all this through Him who gives me strength." God calls us to be women who have joy in our lives and are content with what He has given us. And if your sweet man gave you a box of chocolates for Valentine's Day, be grateful, because there is a woman whose husband forgot the day altogether.

A Holy Woman Is Focused on Her Reality

God has made clear what our purpose on earth is. It is to live a life that glorifies Him. Scripture tell us, "Dear friends, I urge you, as foreigners and exiles, to abstain from sinful desires, which wage war against your soul. Live such good lives among the pagans that, though they accuse you of doing wrong, they may see your good deeds and glorify God on the day he visits us" (1 Peter 2:11–12). Scripture tells us our lives are to be so holy that even the pagans will give glory to God. Often, the sad truth is our Christian sisters cannot glorify God because of the example we set. We cannot expect our unbelieving neighbors or coworkers to be drawn to Christ when they see or hear the ungodliness we allow into our minds. If they see how loosely we hold on to our marriage vows or learn of ways we have compromised, they probably don't see God glorified in our lives.

Our reality is to give God glory through our lives. God has given us our own realities with husbands, kids, families, jobs, sports, schedules, and friends. Sadly, when we entertain false realities, our own realities of marriage and family might be suffering and broken. Rather than investing in our realities, we pour time and energy into false ones. Colossians 3:1–2 says, "Since, then, you have been raised with Christ, set your heart on things above, where Christ is, seated at the right hand of God. Set your mind on things above, not on earthly things." *We need to be women who spend time on the realities of our own marriages, families, and relationships.* We must shift from perceived or false realities to our own realities. Due to the volume of false realities we constantly encounter, this is a choice we must make daily.

A Holy Woman's Mind and Marriage Reflect the Light of Christ

If we are keeping anything a secret from our husbands, whether a fantasy life or an inappropriate relationship, it is a big indicator of potential sin in our lives. If we can't or don't want to share all the details about something with them, it is a red flag. Sin is usually done in darkness. Consider all the sins we secretly do in the dark. Gossip usually starts with a whisper. Lying and deceit aim to suppress the truth or mislead someone. Cheating is going behind someone's back in order to gain for oneself. There is shame and fear in darkness. Nothing about darkness reveals light, which is why we want to keep it hidden. Now contrast darkness with light. We are people of light, and everything in the light is pure, clear, pleasing, and acceptable. *We need to be women whose marriages reflect light because they are a reflection of our thought lives.* Scripture even says, "God is light; in him there is no darkness at all" (1 John 1:5). If our thought lives are not in the light, then we are living contrary to what God says. When we are in emotional sin, we are ineffective for Christ. Our lights cannot shine for Him. We are like candles that have been snuffed out. Matthew 5:14 says, "You are the light of the world." Since God cannot tolerate sin, His reflection cannot be in us when we sin. We actually become the opposite, darkness. We become a poor representation of Christ to a world in desperate need of hope. It's no wonder the unbelieving world is offended by Christians when our lives are often no different from theirs.

A Holy Woman Is Fruitful with Her Thought Life

The sins in our minds are fruitless, and they have negative consequences. Ephesians 5:11–12 says, "Have nothing to do with the fruitless deeds of darkness, but rather expose them. It is shameful even to mention what the disobedient do in secret."

Monica enjoys reading. She used to read romance novels, but recently a friend told her about another novel that she might enjoy. It was racier than Monica was used to, but her friend encouraged her to try it. She and this friend had a lot in common, so she trusted her and agreed. When she went to the bookstore to look for it, the salesclerk told her they would have to order one because they couldn't keep them in stock. When she got her copy and started reading, the book immediately sparked her interest because it was much spicier than the other novels she was used to reading. The book hung on the verge of nastiness, but she could not put it down. She found herself scanning the book for the next part where more illicit sexual descriptions could be found. She often daydreamed about the plot and wondered what would happen next in the fictitious relationship. She would play out the heavy descriptions and often had trouble putting them out of her mind, even when she was with her own husband.

Like Monica, many of us have little fruit in our lives because we have fruitless thought lives. We spend time on something that neither benefits us nor glorifies God. Fruitless thoughts do not help strengthen or restore our marriages, and they don't bring us godly men if we are single. They do not help fix our friendships, and they do not help solve our parenting problems. They are a complete waste of time because whatever predicament we were in before, we are still in after. Often, we are worse off, because fruitless thoughts can cost us time, energy, relationships, and possibly even money. Wasting precious moments of our lives on false realities simply bears no fruit. It is the exact opposite of what we are commanded to do as Christians, which is to bear much fruit. Jesus said in Matthew 7:20, "Thus, by their fruit you will recognize them." *We need to be women who invest wisely with our thought lives.* We reviewed in chapter 3 how our thought lives have direct consequences on our speech, feelings, and actions. A fruitless thought life will affect all areas of our lives.

A Holy Woman Recognizes Evil and Avoids Temptations

Our sin affects this generation and those to come after us. We need to understand that our sinful thought lives will bring bondage for our children. This bondage can carry over for three and four generations. Emotional sins will follow the same route as physical sins. Jeremiah 32:18 says, "You show love to thousands but bring the punishment for the parent's sins into the laps of the children after them." Bondage will affect not only our children but also their families, as well as future generations after them. Satan knows what methods and tactics are effective on us, and he will use the same ones on our children and grandchildren. He won't bother to come up with a new plan for our children when the old plan works effectively on us. The good news is we can break those bondages. We don't have to let our slavery be their slavery. They will have plenty of their own sin to deal with. We should not heap our sin on top of theirs. Every parent wants a better life for his or her children. We should not be satisfied with wanting better for them only financially, academically, or athletically. We should want better for them emotionally as well. Wanting a pure thought life should be just as important, if not more important. Our children should not have to carry yokes they were not meant to carry because we never took the time or effort to deal with our own sin. I cannot think of anything better than a mother who deals with the sin in her own mind so one day her daughter may not have to. What a gift we can give our daughters (and sons). *We need to be women who do not pass on our emotional impurities to our children.*

This is an evil world we live in because it is deeply entrenched in sin. Ephesians 5:15–16 says, "Be very careful, then, how you live—not as unwise but as wise, making the most of every opportunity, because the days are evil." We cannot turn to the left or right without encountering sin. It spills out of our television and computer screens, and it seeps from literature and magazines. Chances are high that no matter what show you turn on or what book you pick up, sin is lurking. Even though it saturates our world, it does not have to saturate our minds. Our lives are short, and the apostle Paul tells us to live as wise people in an evil world. He says to "be efficient with our time." Many of us are efficient when we go to an amusement park. We map out the rides we want to hit first. We plan accordingly with the ones that allow us to skip to the front of the line at a designated time. We eat lunch early to beat the crowd. We walk quickly to other rides during the parade. We leave just before fireworks end to dodge the traffic jam in the parking lot. We need to use the same efficiency with our emotional lives. We must map out, dodge, and walk quickly if we are to avoid evil. We must have a plan. We cannot just expect to avoid it and roll with it when sin comes; rather, we must be actively involved in the pursuit of holiness for our minds. Otherwise the opportunity comes, and we waste it. There is nothing worse than wasting an opportunity, especially on sin. *We need to be women who are efficient in the pursuit of holiness for our minds.*

Genesis 39:10 tells the story of how Joseph resisted temptation—a temptation that is often hard for men to resist. He was like any other young man with hormones and sexual desires when Potiphar's wife tried to seduce him; he refused. Joseph would not entertain the thought of adultery because of his commitment to God and to Potiphar. It must have been an awkward moment for Joseph to walk away from his master's wife while she was propositioning him. He chose awkwardness over sinning against a holy God. He fled from Potiphar's wife when she put the moves on him. Even though she was probably an attractive woman, he fled. He didn't walk, trot, or jog. He fled. Joseph chose his commitment to a holy God over the temptation of sin.

If we constantly saturate our minds with the wrong content from the entertainment world, sin will lurk at our door. Remember, the Enemy prowls around like a lion waiting to devour us. We cannot escape, and we only deceive ourselves if we think we will always be strong enough to resist. If an alcoholic wants to remain sober yet walks into a liquor store, the temptation is hard to resist. Therefore, even the liquor store parking lot should be avoided. We shouldn't trust ourselves either, because we are women with weak emotions and fragile minds. We shouldn't try to prove that we can handle temptation, because we can't. Think of all the times you should have fled from compromising situations. Perhaps it was a movie, a book, a conversation with someone else's husband, or maybe some other "parking lot" that should have been avoided.

If you are stuck in a fantasy life, texting relationship, or pornography, you can get out. You can escape the clutches of sin before it leads to greater harm. If you are having an affair or giving into a destructive addiction, you need to get help. The desire you crave may be real, but you are seeking fulfillment from the wrong place. Getting your emotional needs met from a book, movie, fantasy, or another man is not the plan God designed for you. Holiness is a sacrifice and a process we must choose daily. We must turn from what looks and feels good in exchange for the truth of God's Word. Even if we do not physically engage in sin, that is not enough. We are called to be women who avoid watching, reading, or entertaining sin. God's standards are incredibly high, and ours should be as well.

Chapter 7

Traps and Lies

Do not conform to the pattern of this world, but be transformed by the renewing of your mind. Then you will be able to test and approve what God's will is— his good, pleasing, and perfect will.
—Romans 12:2

As we go through the Christian life, we can often become deceived into thinking that we have "a right to our sin." This is a lie from the pit of hell. There are no entitlements or rights to sin. Romans 6:1–2 says, "What shall we say, then? Shall we go on sinning so that grace may increase? By no means! We are those who have died to sin; how can we live in it any longer?" God hates sin! God does not justify or excuse sin because of our circumstances or unmet needs. A sin is a sin to Him, regardless of our situations. People may do certain things for certain reasons, but sin is never excusable.

I Deserve More or Better

There are people all over this world who live in poverty. Some children live on the streets because their mothers did not survive childbirth, and they have no fathers. These horrors and tragedies are very real and happen every day around the world. When we realize the immensity of others' problems, this puts our own problems into perspective. When we become aware of our situation in light of others, ours often pales in comparison. Women often get stuck in pity parties for ourselves, or we wallow in our sorrows. This is not meant to belittle your problems or to be unsympathetic to your pain. When we hurt, that hurt is our reality, and it is important to us and to God. However, we need to remember there is always someone better off and someone worse off.

We often think if we check all the boxes, our lives will go smoothly. Sometimes we can do all the right things, and life still doesn't go well for us. However, to think that God owes us something because we have made correct choices is prideful. We may think we've done our parts, so now God should do His part. However, God owes us nothing. Anything He gives us is because of His grace and mercy. God never promised us comfortable marriages without marital conflict. He doesn't guarantee us perfect men who will meet our every need. In fact, Jesus said just the opposite. John 16:33 says, "I have told you these things, so that in me you may have peace. In this world you will have trouble. But take heart! I have overcome the world." Life isn't a five-step formula where if we complete one step we are guaranteed the next step. There are no guarantees, even when we have chosen honorably. We will have difficulties in this life in our marriages and other relationships.

Perhaps our husbands aren't romantic enough. Maybe they don't pursue us as they did when we were dating. Maybe they don't make an effort to connect with us emotionally. Maybe they are workaholics or completely consumed with a hobby or sport. Or worse yet, maybe they have completely checked out emotionally or physically. If this is our situation, it can be absolutely devastating, because women are such creatures of emotion. The truth is, it doesn't matter what they have or haven't done. Their actions or inactions do not give us a reason to sin. Two wrongs do not equal a right. Most of us know this, but often we do not apply this principle in marriage. If both marriage partners check out, that spells disaster. If one of them is still holding on, even if by one strand, there is hope and still a lifeline.

Imagine you are stranded with a friend on a rowboat in the middle of the ocean, and each of you has only one oar to paddle with. A few hours later, after not being rescued, your friend tosses her oar into the water in complete despair. Most of us would clutch our oar tighter, knowing it may be our only chance of survival. In marriage, we need to adopt the same standard. We shouldn't toss in our oar when our husband tosses his in. We shouldn't try to meet our needs through sinful avenues and then blame it on our husbands because they failed in doing their part. If you feel neglected in your marriage, whether physically or emotionally, please talk to someone. Ask your church for the name of a godly and respected woman who can listen, pray, and provide counsel. Do not suffer silently. There are many women willing to give of their time to help.

I Married the Wrong Person

At one point, we were attracted to and dated the men we call our husbands. We said yes to first dates, yes to meeting their families, and then yes to their engagement rings. For some of us, waiting for the ring was a long and painful process. We need to remember those beautiful memories. Every one of us wonders at one point if we married "the wrong person." We need to let this be a passing thought and not a thought we constantly entertain. We must be careful not to park our minds on this thought, because it can become consuming and affect other areas of our lives. We must stop wondering if we made a mistake. We often entertain thoughts on how life could have turned out differently or better for us. These thoughts are lies. There are no guarantees. The truth is, our lives could have turned out worse. We must move beyond these thoughts and stop entertaining the should-haves and could-haves. God doesn't make mistakes—not in babies and not in marriages. Any marriage can glorify God when we honor Him, whatever our circumstances. Romans 8:28 says, "He uses all things for the good of those who love Him." He uses all things. Not some things. Not just the good things, but all things, including our marriages. Do not invest time into a reality that didn't happen but rather on the one that did happen. Put those thoughts to rest, and pour your time and energy into loving your husband and meeting his needs. Take note of your husband's positive qualities, and you will start believing your life is better because you are married to him. Be the best that God designed you to be for your husband. Fill his tank to the point that it overflows, so he never has to wonder if he married the wrong person.

It Is Enhancing My Sexual Life

If you are using any kind of pornography or emotional stimulation to enhance your sexual life, it is sin. God created sex between a husband and a wife, not between a person and a magazine, book, or television screen. Despite the appeal of these temptations, it is never acceptable to violate the principles of God in order to receive the blessings of God. There are two great examples in Scripture of violating God's standards to achieve a desired result. The first is with Lot and his daughters. Lot's daughters panicked when they realized they had no children to preserve the family line. Foolishly, they got their father drunk and slept with him (Genesis 19). The second example is in Genesis when God promised a child to Sarah and Abraham. Sarah lacked the faith to believe the child promised to them would come through her because of her old age. She, too, chose foolishly and gave her servant Hagar to Abraham to conceive a child. A child came but not the one promised to them (Genesis 16). The consequences for these women were huge and have continued for generations. The descendants of these two decisions live as enemies to many today. These women's intentions of desiring children were good. Their way of accomplishing their desire was unacceptable and sinful.

God would never ask us to sin to achieve a desired result. Taking matters into our own hands is never a good idea. However, when we take matters into our own hands and it involves sin, it is far worse. Using pornography with our spouses is dishonoring to God and to our husbands. What we are ultimately communicating to our husbands is that they're just not enough. We are telling God what He gave us isn't good enough. Nothing is more degrading and damaging to a marriage than communicating to our husbands that we need more than they have to offer. It would be equally devastating to hear our husbands say they needed other sources of stimulation because we just weren't satisfying them. Regardless of our husbands' shortcomings, we need to communicate that they are perfect fits for us and exactly what we need and desire. We need to demonstrate this through our words and our actions.

Despite any benefits we may experience from using pornography, they are short lived. The dangerous part of any addiction is that the desire for it only increases. We need more of it with more intensity when it no longer satisfies. This leads to bigger issues, and soon we will do whatever it takes to be satisfied. The statistics on women who use pornography (17 percent) indicate the desire for more (see chapter 1). Women who use pornography started somewhere. It started in their minds and eventually led to photos. Even though a woman's first tendency may not be sexual, an emotional sin can turn sexual. Any emotional sin that is well fed and cared for over a period of time can become a physical sin.

Using pornography makes an impression on us now and in the future. It leads us to sinful thoughts when we are with our husbands in the most intimate act. It can also lead us to think about other things during conversations with our husbands. We are supposed to be focused on our husbands when we are with them, not on other things. Pornography can also bring to mind images that may be very hard to shake. Sin takes its toll and leaves a mark behind. The forgiveness of Christ washes it away, but the consequences may follow for a long time. If you are struggling with pornography in your marriage, confess your sin to your husband and to God. Pray and trust God to enhance your emotional and sexual life in your marriage. Talk to your husband and tell him your needs, wishes, and fantasies. After all, he is the one who can turn your fantasy into a reality.

I Am Not Being Unfaithful Physically

The Old Testament was about the law. In the New Testament, Jesus abolished the law and said it was about the intent of the heart. For example, Jesus said, "If you look at a woman lustfully, you have committed adultery in your heart" (Matthew 5:28). Whatever wrong we commit in our hearts, whether it is greed, unkindness, or lust, it is sin. While sin is sin in God's eyes, I often think the manifestation of emotional sin is far worse than physical sin. Emotional sin can make us prideful because we think we are better than others. It's easy to point out the physical sins of others. We deceive ourselves by thinking we haven't done what "they" have. If we really understood sin, we would see that we are no different. While physical sins appear worse and have physical consequences, they are no different from the sin in our heart. The truth is, we are being unfaithful because we have committed the sin in our hearts. We do not need to do something physically to commit sin. And remember, emotional sins may lead to physical sins unless dealt with. A texting relationship with another man may not always remain a texting relationship. One day, it may become a full-fledged affair. When one part of us is in, it is easier for the rest of us to be pulled in. It is much easier to escape the clutches of Satan when he has no part of us. Do not be fooled. Just because you haven't committed the offense physically does not mean you are free from sin.

I'm Single: What's the Harm?

Being single can lead many women to believe they are free from emotional impurity since they are not bound in marriage. While most young, single girls dream of romance, they must be careful their dreams do not cross over into emotional impurity or fantasy lives. One day, God will bring you the man of your dreams; you will fall in love and marry him. You want to be a beautiful bride for him inside and out. Do not be misled into thinking your sexual purity is all that God desires from you. God wants it all, both sexual and emotional purity. Purity for God is a whole package; it's not just one part of you. Do not carry baggage from a sinful thought life into your marriage, because it will affect you. Do not assume that your thought life will automatically stop when you get married. It will carry over, just like any other baggage. When your beautiful and long-awaited day arrives, you need to be investing in your marriage, not sorting out the thoughts that consume you. You want to enjoy the benefits of marriage and offer your husband your best. If you already have emotional baggage, it is better to deal with it now when you have the time and freedom from marital responsibilities. God desires you to keep yourself emotionally and physically pure. No matter how long the wait, the rewards and benefits will be worth it. There will be eternal value with blessings for you and your children.

Many of you who find yourself single once again, must adopt this same standard of emotional purity. Whether your desire is to marry again or to remain single does not make a difference. God's standard of holiness does not change based on our circumstances. He still commands us to the pursuit of holiness both physically and emotionally. Regardless of how you feel about being single, your situation may change. And if it does, it is best to be in obedience.

We must realize that when we choose sin, we will have consequences. Sometimes the consequences come in the future and are not immediate, but either way, we cannot escape them. Our sin is not limited to us alone. It will affect those around us as well. Sin is like an earthquake, sending rippling waves in a circle around us. The worst effects are felt by the people closest to us, yet sin still radiates to those we come in contact with. Often, sin's effects go deeper and wider, affecting people we may never even know.

Chapter 8

The Pretty Temptation

And the peace of God, which transcends all understanding, will guard your hearts and minds in Christ Jesus. Finally brothers and sisters, whatever is true, whatever is noble, whatever is right, whatever is pure, whatever is lovely, whatever is admirable—if anything is excellent or praiseworthy—think about such things.

—Philippians 4:7–8

When Jesus was in the wilderness and had been fasting for forty days and nights, Satan came to tempt Him (Matthew 4). It was an almost perfect temptation and one we can learn from—not because Satan is perfect, as he is not even close. Satan knew how to attack Jesus where it hurt the most. He used ordinary things wrapped up in pretty packages to tempt Jesus. Satan often does the same with us. He knows what tactics worked on our mothers and grandmothers, and he knows which ones will work for us. Jesus provided us with the perfect example of how we should respond when we are faced with temptation. Our circumstances may line up just the right way for temptation, but we do not have to succumb to sin. There is always a way out. No matter what previous generations have passed down to us, we still are responsible for the choices we make. God has given us the Holy Spirit to perfectly guide and instruct us, no matter the temptation.

Satan Appeals to Our Most Basic Needs

Jesus' first temptation involved Satan's invitation to turn stones into bread. At first glance, it doesn't seem much like a temptation. Matthew 4:2–3 says, "After fasting forty days and forty nights, he was hungry. The tempter came to him and said, 'If you are the Son of God, tell these stones to become bread.'" Jesus had been without food for forty days. Because He was fully human, He was hungry. Satan knew Jesus was famished and viciously attacked Him. It was a malicious attempt by Satan to destroy Jesus in a vulnerable moment.

Satan often appeals to women's basic needs, just as he appealed to Jesus with hunger. When basic needs are not met, we become frustrated, irritable, and sometimes desperate. Anytime we are desperate, we are fragile and vulnerable. We are open and ready to listen to anything that might satisfy our unmet need. It is similar to being the new kid in school who is desperate for some friends. Whichever crowd accepts or reaches out first is the group the kid will most likely follow. The kid will listen and may even follow the wrong crowd just out of the desire to gain some friends. Many times, in our desperation, we also follow and listen to whomever and whatever.

As women, our emotional needs include love, romance, touch, acceptance, companionship, communication, and feeling desirable. If these emotional needs are not met, we are prime candidates for an attack from the Enemy. Satan is well aware of our need for these things from our husbands. If we don't get them, we are vulnerable and fertile ground just waiting to be invaded. Satan purposively attacks us with evil right where it hurts. He will lead us to believe it is acceptable to turn on romantic feelings for another man, whether through a movie or when a friend's husband has taken an interest in us. Satan will attempt to deceive us into believing it is okay to read explicit sexual details in a book or to communicate extensively with the opposite sex on social media even though we are married. For those who are not yet married, he will lead you to think it is acceptable to receive romance from inappropriate sources. Regardless of how good these things may make us feel, none of the above is acceptable. We must recognize our vulnerability because of our unmet needs. We need to know it is sinful and unacceptable to meet these needs through movies, television shows, books, fantasies, or through social outlets with other men. We should receive love and acceptance from our husbands only. However, if we do not, we must not compromise holiness and seek unholy sources. Jesus knew that however good and desirable the bread would look and taste, He could not compromise His holiness to meet His immediate unmet need. In the same way, we cannot compromise holiness for our unmet emotional needs either.

Satan Uses Ordinary and Good Things

Satan used something very ordinary in his efforts to tempt Jesus. He used stones. Stones are certainly not sinful, and turning stones into bread is not sinful either. After all, Jesus turned water into wine, and it was called a miracle. The sin wasn't in the stone or bread; it was using the stone for the wrong purpose. Satan was tempting Jesus to meet His need of hunger by using the stone incorrectly. Different forms of media in our lives may not be sinful, although there is plenty of sin in them. Rather, it is how we use the media and for what purpose. Anything ordinary and good can become sinful when used inappropriately. When we take these ordinary and good media and use them incorrectly to satisfy needs, it is sin. Romance movies are not meant to replace romance in our marriages. Cell phones are not meant to replace communication with our husbands. The bread would have never satisfied Jesus because His true hunger was for the Word of God. Whatever we use inappropriately will never satisfy us either.

Satan Feeds Us Conditional Lines

Satan told Jesus that God would save Him if He jumped down from the temple. Matthew 4:5–6 says, "Then the devil took him to the holy city and had him stand on the highest point of the temple. 'If you are the Son of God,' he said, 'Throw yourself down.'" Notice how Satan fed Jesus a conditional line: "If you are who you say you are, then you will do this." It is an "if then" statement, pointing out that a certain set of conditions applies based on one's circumstance or status. Satan does the same with us. He feeds us "if then" statements all the time. He uses lines, such as "If you are married, then you deserve ..." or "Since you're not married, you can engage in ..." and so on. Satan does a fine job of pointing out our statuses and selling us on the privileges that apply to them. He tries to convince us we have rights based on our statuses. Regardless of our marital statuses or circumstances, we do not have a right to sin.

Satan Has *Nothing* to Offer Us

In the third temptation, Satan offered Jesus power and riches if He would bow down and worship him. Matthew 4:8–9 says, "Again the devil took him to a very high mountain and showed him all the kingdoms of the world and their splendor. 'All this I will give you,' he said, 'if you will bow down and worship me.'" Satan tried to convince Jesus that if He would worship him, he would give Him all the power in the world. The irony is Satan had absolutely nothing to offer Jesus. How foolish he was to even think he had anything to offer. Jesus already had all the power. Satan has *nothing* to offer us either. He never has, and he never will. Nothing he flashes in front of our eyes is of enduring value or worth. Nothing he offers us is even worthwhile to consider.

Jesus knew Satan could not give Him power. He knew Satan and his schemes. We are often misled with offers of power also. For women, power is often summed up in a little word, *control*. The power may come from taking control of a situation in our marriages through our own measures. Single women can also try to control their circumstances of wanting a boyfriend or husband. We feel when we can manipulate or control something, we are in charge. The irony is, we really aren't in control, no matter what we may think or feel. God is ultimately the one in charge of our marriages or single lives. He is the only one who has the power to change them. Anything God offers us is worthwhile and of lasting value.

Satan Tries to Convince Us That Sin Will Satisfy

Satan also tried to convince Jesus that gaining the kingdoms of the world would somehow satisfy Him. As if all the riches in the world would bring some sort of gratification to Jesus! Satan does the same with us. He leads us to believe that if we follow him, our needs and desires will somehow be met. He cunningly leads us to believe that sin will satisfy us, and then we will be fine. He works to make us believe that sin will solve our problems. We sometimes believe his lies that our marriages will be fixed when we resort to our own methods. He convinces us that if we had just that "one thing," we would have a sense of contentment. Unmet needs and desires will never be satisfied with sin. Sin does just the opposite. It only leads to more hunger and more sin. If sin truly satisfied, we would be content and go back to our normal lives. Just like the bread Satan offered Jesus, sin does not solve our problem; it provides only momentary satisfaction. The truth is that "one thing" won't satisfy us either.

Satan Tries to Make Sin Look Pretty

Satan tried to convince Jesus what He could have by showing Him "all the kingdoms of the world and their splendor." It must have been a beautiful view from the mountaintop for Jesus. Often, Satan gives us a taste of the thing we may be craving through a small taste or glimpse. He dangles the bait close enough for us to see. He tries to show us what we are missing and lets us sample his offerings until one really appeals to us. He then targets us in that particular area. Temptation is not "one size fits all." This is why women can struggle with different issues. No matter how good Satan makes a temptation seem, it is not true. No matter how good he makes it look, it is a lie. Satan has a crafty way of making sin appear so wonderful. Since women like pretty things, we often are lured into believing something beautiful must be good. Satan knows that presentation is everything. He knows how to make sin shiny and pretty for us. Everything shiny and pretty isn't always good or safe.

Sometimes our circumstances in life make us perfect targets of the Enemy. Sometimes this is our own doing, and sometimes it is not. In the next chapter, we will discuss some potential triggers that make women particularly vulnerable to temptation. Before you read further, take a moment to think about where you have unmet needs in your life, especially in your marriage. If you are single, evaluate what things you long for and desire. These are areas Satan will likely try to use and try to satisfy in sinful ways. When we are aware of our vulnerabilities, we will have more discernment to resist possible temptations. This brings us one step closer to being victorious in our emotional purity.

Chapter 9

Roller Coasters

Submit yourselves, then to God. Resist the devil, and
he will flee from you. Come near to God and he will
come near to you. Wash your hands, you sinners, and
purify your hearts, you double-minded.

—James 4:7–8

Roller coasters are thrilling for some people, but for others they are scary. Some are mild, and some are extremely intense. Sometimes when we hop on a roller coaster, we have no idea what we may encounter. As women, we are often like roller coasters with our emotions. One moment we are up, and the next we are down, spiraling through the air unsure of where we will land. We laugh, we cry, and sometimes we don't know what to do or how to feel. There are certain moments when we are fine, and then there are other moments when we are a complete mess. Our hormones fluctuate with our cycles and can wreak emotional havoc on our minds. There are also other triggers that come from the world. These triggers can also make our emotions fluctuate.

With our constantly changing technology, there will always be a "latest and best" technology for us to test or own. We cannot control the things from the world, but we can choose how we will use them and how we will allow them to influence our minds. We have incredible relational needs that most men don't have and don't understand. All of these triggers can make us vulnerable and weak when confronted by the Enemy. This can happen when conditions are right in our lives, both physically and emotionally. Sometimes all it takes is one trigger, but often it is a combination of triggers. We need to be fully alert and take note of them because they can become Satan's stomping ground. If we are not careful, he can use our emotions to lure us into sin during these moments.

Menstrual Cycle

It is amazing that a natural bodily occurrence can affect us so deeply. Every woman knows that her emotions can greatly correlate with her menstrual cycle. Typically, we are very emotional creatures the days before and during our periods. Simple and silly things can trigger us to cry. Our husbands do not understand us during this time (do they ever really understand us?) and usually just keep their distance to avoid any unnecessary tears. During this time, we usually want tenderness, sweetness, and to be held by the men in our lives. We can be crampy, irritable, and completely irrational.

Unlike our levelheaded husbands, we often are not rational at all during our periods. We can do crazy things and think irrational thoughts, and Satan can have a field day with our emotions. He uses anything he can to entice, captivate, and lure our vulnerable hearts. We have to be careful not to let our emotions guide us, no matter how strong they may be. Rather, we must turn to the truth of God's Word and remind ourselves not to feed our feelings, because they will change in a few days.

Sometime during the seven days following our periods, we ovulate. Our emotions make a complete turn, and we shift from being irritable to desiring romance. If our husbands do not meet our romantic needs during this time, it can lead us to meet them by other means. We may turn to a fantasy, a romantic movie, or another source to fill this desire. Be sure to take action in guarding your heart and emotions; do not just sit back and expect holy behavior to happen on its own. It might mean avoiding a certain show or avoiding television altogether. It might mean avoiding a place or a certain someone. It will look different for every woman depending on her situation, so be sure not to judge a sister because she is doing something different from you. Take the necessary steps, and guard your heart.

Husbands

These are times when we experience difficulty with our husbands. The cause can be a fight, stress over finances or parenting, or our suspicion that our husbands are intentionally or unintentionally ignoring our emotional, relational, or sexual needs. That lack of emotional and relational attention can be devastating because of the way we are wired. There is an equal devastation when we are ignored sexually. Regardless of how much we say we don't need or can live without sex, we want our husbands to find us desirable and beautiful. The type of rejection doesn't matter when it comes to our husbands because we interpret any rejection as the ultimate rejection when it comes from them. For some of us, we were rejected by our fathers or lost our fathers, so we expect our husbands to fulfill that nurturing and loving role. Or perhaps our earthly fathers were loving and present in our lives, but we still expect our husbands to be our heroes and our rescuers. When our husbands don't fulfill these expectations, we can be crushed and devastated. The need for communication and compliments is so strong that it can lead us to seek to fulfill these needs in destructive ways. The romance in television shows may appeal to us because of our desire to be pursued. We secretly long to be the woman whose husband valiantly pursues her. We want him to fight, protect, and ultimately rescue us. But some husbands may not budge from the couch, much less climb up on a horse.

God did design us to be sought after, protected, and rescued. We seek this from men, usually our husbands. Yes, our husbands should be willing to fight for us, protect us, and die for us. But ultimately, they are not our rescuers. Jesus is our fighter, protector, and rescuer. No husband, no matter how wonderful he may be, can fulfill the role Jesus came to fulfill. Whatever the disappointment or stress may be with our husbands, this does not justify meeting our needs from other sources. We must be vigilant to protect ourselves from sources that will "romance" us, especially if our husbands do not.

Loneliness

There is no doubt that loneliness and hurt can often lead us to unhealthy habits. While some turn to food or alcohol, others may turn to a television show, a book, a fantasy, or another relationship. We so desperately want to fill the gap of loneliness that we reach for something that will satisfy it. Once again, any satisfaction we receive is temporary, especially if the loneliness is the result of a husband who communicates infrequently or not at all. We were designed to be emotional and relational. We want to sit down with our husbands and have a conversation. We want them to ask about our days, and we want to hear about theirs. We want them to come home and tell us the exact details when their coworker has a baby. Early on in my marriage, this happened to us when my husband came home from work and informed me that his colleague's wife had had their baby. I asked what I thought were the normal questions: name, weight, length, and status of the mother. He didn't know any of the answers, and I was horrified. All my husband knew was that the baby was born alive and that the mother probably was still alive as well. It was enough information for him, and he didn't realize that I wanted more. The next time someone had a baby, he brought a note home on which he had scribbled all the details and handed it to me. I was elated because he took note of what was important to me and responded. I learned something important that day as a new bride. What matters to me doesn't necessarily matter to him. Most women and men are relationally different. We need to be careful we do not misinterpret our husbands' relational qualities. Just because they don't communicate in the manner and frequency we would like does not mean they don't love us.

Occasionally, my husband takes our daughter out on a dinner date. During one of those evenings, he glanced at his cell phone during dinner. Before he could even look up, she said,

"I thought we were going to have a conversation, Dad." Most women love to communicate. Sometimes we talk just to express our thoughts, but we also crave the connectedness that verbal communication brings.

Loneliness can come from a lack of girlfriends as well and can be equally as strong. When this desire for connectedness is not met, we can seek it from the wrong places or the wrong people. Compliments from another man, conversations with the opposite sex, or texting in an ongoing way with another man becomes so meaningful because we long for constant verbal communication with our husbands. These are the wrong avenues to seek and find connectedness. We may get the words and the compliments we desire, but these are not God's intended sources for connectedness. They can quickly take us down a very dangerous and destructive path that is hard to escape.

Friends

Sometimes the people we associate with can lead us into temptation. You know, the ones we often call our friends. The people we rub shoulders with will do one of two things. They will either build us up or tear us down. It doesn't necessarily have to be with words; it can also be with the influence of their lives. The friends in our lives should be such that they build us up, encourage us, and inspire us. We should be better people because of them. They don't have to be perfect; they just have to be people striving to live for Jesus with character and integrity. When they make mistakes or sin, they recognize it and reveal broken and repentant spirits. The people we associate with have a tremendous impact on us, and we need to be careful that they are the right kind of people who rightly influence us. This influence is more important than ever during our moments of weakness. Proverbs 12:26 says, "The righteous choose friends carefully, but the way of the wicked leads them astray." We need friends who are bold enough to confront us and tell us we are going against God's standards. We need friends who have strong convictions to point out our errors and steer us in the right direction.

If you have friends in your life who are not a positive spiritual influence, you need to set up boundaries with them. One boundary would be not to seek counsel or advice from them. If they are not living for Jesus, they have nothing to offer you in the spiritual realm. On the contrary, they can only give you worldly counsel based on feelings and emotions. That is a self-centered approach that causes confusion and can cloud our thinking, possibly leading us to make unwise and destructive decisions. If you confide in a friend that you are secretly involved in a texting relationship with another man, she might wrongly encourage you, for example, since she is operating from a worldly perspective.

Some friendships may need to be severed altogether, especially if their influence is detrimental. This may include the popular friend who gets invited to every event, who dresses really cute, and who appears to have it all by the standards of the world. If we find ourselves succumbing to her negative influence or dwelling on worldly desires, then hers is a destructive friendship. Perhaps a friend encourages us to read a pornographic novel or is married and wants us to accompany her to questionable places. If we tend to cave under that kind of pressure, we need to walk away from the friendship and choose God and our husbands over the friend. God will honor us and our marriages for honoring Him. Listen to what Deuteronomy 13:6–8 says: "If your very own brother, or your son or daughter, or the wife you love, or your closest friend, secretly entices you saying, 'Let us go worship other gods' (gods that neither you nor your ancestors have known, gods of the peoples around you, whether near or far, from one end of the land to the other), do not yield to them or listen to them. Show them no pity." God commanded the Israelites to not surround themselves with people from other nations because they were a holy people. He expects the same from us, to be women set apart even with our friendships.

Choosing holiness may be very lonely, but we must always choose holiness, even at the cost of friendships. We, as women, sometimes equate our worth with the measure of our social lives, yet Jesus never preached about popularity. He never once taught us how to be part of the "in crowd." He did just the opposite when He instructed us on loving the least of these … the unlovable, the unpopular, and those the world rejects. It is difficult, because women want to have the "cool friends" and long to be included. We want to be invited to the parties and accepted so badly we will go to extreme measures to fit in. Jesus was often found alone because holiness can be a lonely journey. He had a small group of friends. Most of the time, He was not popular but hated even to the point of death. Remember, holiness is a tight squeeze, not a five-lane highway.

Jesus has taught me the most in my moments of extreme loneliness. A wise friend once told me, "Holiness is sometimes walking single file alone with Jesus, with no one on the left or the right." Holiness is usually not found in a crowded room but rather one-on-one with our Savior. Holiness does not and should not equate with being popular in the world we live in.

Do not make the mistake of thinking you can be the "good Christian" living in the midst of only non-Christian friends. If unbelievers are the only ones you run in circles with, you may be headed for trouble. I am not implying that you shouldn't rub shoulders with, influence, or minister to unbelievers. I am saying that they shouldn't be your only source of friendship. Not only do they have nothing to offer you spiritually, but their lifestyles will usually not exemplify holy living. You need to check whether you are doing the influencing rather than being the one influenced. If you aren't the one doing the influencing, you need to back off the relationship. You must surround yourself with godly people if you are to live a godly life. You must have an influence of holiness if you are to live a holy life. We must be women who have godly women in our lives to point us to Christ. We would never allow our children to associate only with kids who were a negative influence on them; we should set the same guidelines for ourselves.

Sometimes we will lose friends when we choose holiness. Women tend to think that a severed friendship means we have done something wrong. It can sometimes lead us to a guilt trip. Don't make that mistake. If the friendship is broken because of different lifestyles, then any guilt we may feel is false. We can invite and encourage someone to live in our world, but we should never live in hers. Offending some friends may be unavoidable. Jesus offended people when He spoke the truth of God's Word. He didn't come to make best friends with everyone or to be the most well liked guy around. If we unintentionally offend by choosing to live differently from the world around us, then we shouldn't beat ourselves up. We need to be more concerned about the high standard Christ has called us to and less concerned about what others think.

Media

The influence of television entertainment alone is captivating and enticing. Hearing about the popular series everyone is watching or a show with worldly values is hard to avoid today. The latest movie releases promise romance but often promote adultery, cheating, lying, and sneaking around. If there is not outright adultery, there is usually an underlying theme of sexual looseness. Profanity seems to drip from the actors' mouths as if it is their second language. Even the clothes worn by actresses are very revealing, and sex is treated like a casual encounter. The sexual forwardness of the actresses is frightening. It is a poor influence on us and on our daughters to think the ways to attract a man are through sexual boldness and skimpy clothing.

Watching a movie or show with grand romantic gestures can breed discontentment with our own spouses and marriages. We set our husbands up for failure when they cannot possibly live up to the unrealistic expectations painted for them on the television or movie screens. I don't know too many women who get a room filled with roses or who are whisked off to Paris by private jet at a moment's notice.

The reality shows portrayed today are at a record high. Everything and everyone seems to have a show based on their "reality." Some portray a picture-perfect life of luxury cars, big houses, fancy vacations, career-climbing parents, and super athletic kids. Others depict a real-life mess filled with drama and heartache. We set ourselves up for failure with either of these shows. We either are discontented due to viewing someone else's "perfect life," or we ride the wave of watching someone's misery unfold. Watching addictive behavior destroy one's life or seeing a young child receive a wedding-sized birthday party cannot be beneficial for us. We have enough drama of our own to contend with. We do not need to watch it unfold for others.

Social media has an impact on our lives like never before. It is a double-edged sword with many benefits and deadly risks. With email and Internet, it is easier than ever to locate a close restaurant or a phone number you need while running errands. It's also easier than ever to find someone to connect with— sometimes the wrong someone. All it takes is a few strokes of a device to send a message to someone of the opposite sex. What may or may not start out as an innocent message or text can quickly grow into a lengthy conversation or relationship that is easily justified.

Technology is a challenge. It is often used to communicate schedules, cancellations, and appointments. It serves a wonderful purpose, but even the right intentions can be used to lure us in. It's amazing how quickly words can shift from sports or school to another topic. Remember, the Enemy lures with deceit. He makes us believe one little comment we make or receive can't hurt us. He makes us think that one taste of the forbidden fruit is acceptable. Be cautious when using technology for communication purposes with the opposite sex. If you feel an attraction, or if things get uncomfortable, or if you feel the least bit suspicious, have your husband respond or turn to another avenue to communicate. Stick to the original purpose of the message. When the intent was to communicate about a soccer game cancellation, texting about other matters is not a good idea.

We should also be very cautious when communicating with men from our past relationships. Most of us would not want our husbands in touch with their old girlfriends. Keeping relationships alive from our past isn't necessary. Nothing good can come from reaching out to an old boyfriend. Our husbands' permission should always be sought. If you are friendly with a man from your past, avoid personal or private messages. Stick to general topics and always keep your husband informed of your conversations.

Women also tend to be very bold with their comments on social media. Things that would never be said in public conversations are strongly stated behind the curtain of a computer screen. Every comment does not need to be shared; some things are better left unsaid. We need to eliminate the desire to comment or leave a post on everything. The "who's done what and with whom" mentality is not healthy either. Some women find their worth through being in the know. Letting everyone know what we did last night or sharing where we are going to eat dinner tonight often only screams of pride. We always want to "one up" someone. Most of the time, the person we try to "one up" is someone who we haven't seen in years or lives in another state. We want our "friends" to know our lives are a big deal and we matter. It's about self-promotion.

We do matter. However, our worth as women is only found in Jesus and not because someone in another state knows where we vacationed last summer. Everything in our lives should not be made public. We need to keep some things private. Some matters are meant only for our husbands and us, some are meant only for close friends, and some are meant only for us. Before you decide to share, evaluate your motives for doing so. Ask yourself, *is this meant to share what I have been blessed with, or is all about advertising myself?*

Music is another media source that tends to grab our attention. While music can be beautiful and relaxing, it can also be captivating. Just like television and movies, some secular lyrics are laced with immorality, cheating, and lust. Even the music videos can be sexually explicit. Music can also stimulate us emotionally, especially if it brings back memories from the past with old boyfriends. It may lead us to fantasize about them or about the time spent with them. Take some times to read the lyrics of your favorite hit song to understand what the message is really about, and evaluate where it is taking you in your mind.

Literature

Women have become a huge target of novels lately. Novels have evolved from romance to literature with racy themes and descriptive sexual content. These racy novels, which emotionally appeal to women, are pornography for women. We cannot point fingers at our husbands and then feel no conviction when we read about explicit sexual acts ourselves. Some are not just sexual acts but vulgar and brutal sexual acts that devalue women and remove every ounce of love and romance from the relationship. These themes also completely distort the marriage relationship. Marriage is symbolic of Christ's love for the church. He suffered and died for the church. God provided the ultimate example of how a marriage relationship should work with Christ as the groom and the church as the bride. Christ loves the church and gently woos her to Him. This teaches husbands how to love their wives and how wives should respect their husbands in return. The vulgarity in these books taints the gospel and puts an ugly spin on marriage. It is a completely inaccurate representation of God's intention for marriage. We cannot stand in support of these types of novels, and we need to speak up about the harm they can do.

Romance novels, however mild and innocent they may seem, can be equally tempting. They have the ability to take us on a journey that gratifies us emotionally and romantically. If our emotional appetite is satisfied through them, that is sin. There is a fine line between whether we are reading them for pure enjoyment or because we are lacking emotionally. Ask yourself if you are reading these types of books for a good story or to meet a deep emotional need.

Reading magazines can be another dangerous avenue. Magazines are filled with articles promoting sexual promiscuity and compromising photos. Even the question and answer columns speak of immorality in a "do what feels good" mentality. We easily get lured in with captivating headlines on articles promising us answers to our problems. Most of these magazines are based on a worldly perspective and have little to offer us spiritually.

Victory

Moments of victory can also make us vulnerable to attack if we are not careful. These are times when all is well, and we have mountaintop experiences. Being the sinful humans we are, we pride ourselves into thinking we do not need God when things go well for us. Proverbs 16:18 says, "Pride goes before destruction, a haughty spirit before a fall." Scripture warns us that when pride puffs up our egos, we become too confident. Pride prevents us from recognizing danger. Our relationships with our husbands may be at an all-time high, but we must be vigilant constantly. We cannot park our minds in neutral and expect things to keep going well. Marriages, like anything else worthwhile, take work. We must continue to put forth time, effort, and energy. Eventually there will be a fight, disagreement, or marital stress. We will encounter difficulties in this world, and the key is to be ready when they come.

Normal

Sometimes the normal routines of life become mundane, and we become complacent. A friend reminded me of a great example of this when she backed her car into something, damaging her rear bumper. She has a fancy car with a rearview camera that beeps when you get too close to something. It's not that she didn't hear the beeping noise. She did. She had become so used to it when backing out that she no longer paid attention to it. It was warning her she was too close to something, and she failed to notice. How often do we have normal boundaries and guardrails in our lives that we tend to brush off when they are actually a warning to be heeded? Sometimes life is boring, routine, and normal, but that doesn't guarantee we are safe. Pay attention to those warnings. Satan uses opportunities like these to catch us off guard. Don't let the normal and good boundaries we have installed become so routine that we completely ignore them. Many of us have fences in our backyards for safety reasons. Fences protect what we own and keep out intruders. When the gate is left open, the fence is of limited benefit. It cannot serve its primary purpose of protection because it has been breached. The same is true with boundaries. They only work when they are used properly. Take a moment and think of the boundaries in your life, realizing they are for your protection. If you don't have them, you need to establish them. And next time you back up in your car, pay attention to the beeping!

Roller coaster moments come in many different ways. They differ from one woman to the next. While one is a real trigger for someone, it may not be an issue for another. Please take a moment to prayerfully consider which ones affect you. Which moments lead you to a place where you may compromise emotionally? If you are having difficulty, take the time to journal when you feel vulnerable, and you might discover a pattern. We take great care to prepare our kids for the dangers they will face with drugs, alcohol, tobacco use, and premarital sex. In the same way, we need to prepare ourselves for the dangers that lurk around us. In the next chapter, we will examine how God wants us to respond to temptations and to sin.

Chapter 10

Guard Your Heart

I have hidden your word in my heart that I might not sin against you.

—Psalm 119:11

Be Rude in the Face of Sin

As women, we always try to be the "nice girl" because we don't want to be rude. We should be nice girls. God desires us to be women who honor Him and love others. However, too many of us are nice to the wrong things. The world screams immorality to us from every source. Worldly sources boldly speak their standards, and we very timidly avoid offending anyone. We tiptoe or skirt around issues because we don't want anyone to "take it the wrong way."

Jesus Himself was angry when an injustice was taking place in His temple, flipping over tables and knocking things to the ground (Matthew 21:13). He came not to please people but to teach the truth. He didn't care what people thought of Him; He was there to do the will of His Father. God has given us permission to be rude with sin also. As Scripture says, "Flee from sexual immorality" (1 Corinthians 6:18). Running from sin can be interpreted by others as rude. God does want us to treat people well, but if a person is the source of our temptation, we need to lace up our running shoes. God knows our intentions and that we are running from the temptation and not from the person. When an inappropriate relationship with another man has gone on way too long, whether we feel convicted or not, we need to just walk away. We don't need to explain, defend, or even apologize. We need to walk in the other direction. In these situations, it's better to be rude in the face of sin. When the conversation on a social media outlet turns sexual, we need to close our accounts. We don't need to explain why we "unfriended" someone or why we are shutting it down. Be rude in the face of sin. The temptation is too great to leave accounts open because most women feel the need to explain themselves. This only draws out the situation and may pull us back in.

Whether we need to change our cell phone number, close down an Internet page, or change an email address, we must do it. We may need to stop frequenting a certain store or eating at a certain restaurant. We may need to change doctors or dentists. It may cost us financially or relationally, but it doesn't matter. It doesn't matter what others think or how we will be perceived. When our marriages are at stake, we should be willing to take whatever measures we need to protect them. These measures are a small price to pay to protect our marriages and families. We need to be rude in the face of sin and not feel as if we need to be the "nice girl" in these situations.

Even Jesus spoke about resorting to extreme measures when dealing with sin. Matthew 5:29–30 says, "If your right eye causes you to stumble, gouge it out and throw it away. It is better for you to lose one part of your body than for your whole body to be thrown into hell. And if your right hand causes you to stumble, cut it off and throw it away. It is better for you to lose one part of your body than for your whole body to go into hell." Whatever or whomever is standing in the way of our holiness must be removed. It is a requirement, not an option.

Respond with Scripture

Earlier we discussed how Jesus was tempted; now we will focus on how He responded to the temptation. Jesus has given us the ultimate example of how to respond when confronted with sin. He handled temptation perfectly. To set the stage, Jesus was led by the Spirit of God into the wilderness and fasted for forty days and nights. He was alone, and He was hungry. Satan tempted Jesus three different times. Each time Jesus responded with Scripture. Jesus didn't rationalize or ask questions. He was firm and direct when He quoted Scripture to Satan. He showed great strength and confidence in what He said. God offers the same confidence to us. It is through Him we are strong, not in ourselves: "My power is made perfect in weakness, for my grace is sufficient for you" (2 Corinthians 12:9). We can be confident because God is our confidence. We need to have Scripture memorized for times like this when the Enemy comes after us. We can't be fumbling with our words. We need to confidently proclaim the promises of God. We need to boldly believe in those promises. If you lack the faith to believe what He has promised, ask Him to give you the faith to believe them.

In the back of this book, there is a list of Scripture verses pertaining to the heart and to the mind. Pick one for per week and write it on a notecard or in a journal. Tape a notecard to your ceiling so it is the last thing you see before going to bed and the first thing you see when you wake up. Tape it to your bathroom mirror so you can be reminded of God's Word as you apply your makeup and fix your hair. Say it certain times throughout the day when you are stopped at a red light or when you are picking up your cell phone. Tape a copy to your steering wheel as a reminder to keep your feet from running or driving to evil. Stick one on the television remote control or on the computer screen to prompt you to make wise choices regarding what you see and do. Surround your things or places of greatest temptation with Scripture so your mind can be constantly reminded of the truth of God's Word.

We often underestimate the power of God's Word because we don't really understand the power behind it. With His words, God created the world and breathed life into humans. God spoke, and it was. With His words, Jesus turned water into wine, healed the sick, and raised people from the dead. Hebrews 4:12 says, "For the word of God is alive and active. Sharper than any double-edged sword, it penetrates even to dividing soul and spirit, joints and marrow; it judges the thoughts and attitudes of the heart." A double-edged sword is a sword with blades on both sides. When used, it cuts both ways. It cuts the person it is meant for, and the back swing of the sword cuts the one using it. Scripture tells us God's words are sharper than any double-edged sword. They are living, and when applied, they penetrate deep into our hearts. His words always cut, molding and shaping us into to the likeness of Christ. Scripture is extremely powerful and is our weapon for fighting the Enemy. We will never effectively win the battle over our temptations without using Scripture.

God's Word says, "All scripture is God-breathed and is useful for teaching, rebuking, correcting, and training in righteousness" (2 Timothy 3:16). Scripture is designed for the purpose of benefitting our Christian walk in many areas. One of them is for correction, which applies to ourselves and others. God's Word will penetrate our minds and correct our thought lives. It takes our thoughts and lines them up according to God's standards. It is like a compass that points us in the right direction. Another purpose of Scripture is for training in righteousness; which is living a holy life. His Word displays His character and attributes to demonstrate how we are to live as imitators of Him. We cannot be imitators of Him without Scripture.

It is not enough to just know God, but we must know His Word too. To just know God is like saying you know the Queen of England. You may know her, but you know nothing about her likes or dislikes. You have no idea what her favorite color or food is. You know about her in a very general sense, but you are not intimately involved in her life. When we read Scripture, we get to know God on a very intimate level. We understand what His favorite color is (and it isn't gray), what He loves, and what He hates. It is only when we are intimately involved with Him that we can we become imitators of Him. To know God is to know His Word. It is not possible to know one without the other. Ephesians 6:11–17 says,

> Put on the full armor of God, so you can take your stand against the devil's schemes. For our struggle is not against flesh and blood, but against the rulers, against the authorities, against the powers of this dark world and against the spiritual forces of evil in the heavenly realms.

> Therefore put on the full armor of God, so that
> when the day of evil comes, so you may be able
> to stand your ground, and after you have done
> everything, to stand. Stand firm then with the
> belt of truth buckled around your waist, with
> the breastplate of righteousness of place, and
> your feet fitted with the readiness that comes
> from the gospel of peace. In addition to all this,
> take up the sword of faith, with which you can
> extinguish all the flaming arrows of the evil
> one. Take the helmet of salvation and the sword
> of the spirit, which is the word of God.

We need the Word of God to effectively and purposively fight our battles.

We need to be like Jesus. If Jesus used Scripture to fight the Enemy, how can we use anything but Scripture? We have nothing in and of ourselves to fight with. God offers us everything we need to fight the Enemy, but we must rely on Him and His Word.

Don't Entertain the Enemy

Jesus didn't pause and wait for a response from Satan. He didn't even give Satan an opportunity for a comeback. We shouldn't entertain the Enemy either. We shouldn't engage him in conversation. We shouldn't engage in a question and answer session with him. We must know our Enemy and his corrupt ways. He cheats and lies. He doesn't play by the rules. He is our worst opponent because he doesn't play fair. He never tries to see things our way and has no intention of working it out. Too often we seek advice from well-meaning friends, and sometimes the wrong friends give us the wrong advice. We get together for coffee, and everyone offers her two cents about our situation. We ask questions like, "What do you think?" and "What would you do if you were in my shoes?" Some advise us that what we are doing or contemplating is acceptable because we "deserve more" than our husbands "can give us." Some may tell us, "If it's helping your marriage, it must be fine." We listen to them tell stories of what their neighbors are doing, and we don't feel so bad after all. We leave feeling pretty good because they justify our sin. We look around and see other Christian women reading the same book and think, "If so and so can read it, then I can too." If we are doing something wrong, we don't need to ask our girlfriends what they think. It matters what a holy God thinks. We do not need human counsel when the Holy Spirit has convicted us of sin. Sometimes a friend cannot allow herself to feel convicted because she may be condemning herself if she has a similar struggle. If anyone gives us different advice when we have been convicted, we need to be obedient to what God is asking of us. Our actions from our convictions will speak volumes to those around us.

Contrast Jesus' response to Eve's response in the garden. We all know the story of how the serpent came to her after God commanded her and Adam not to eat from one tree. The serpent asked Eve a question, and she answered him. She entertained him one time, and next she knew, she was in a full-blown conversation with the Devil. Satan is cunning, and he knows how to lure us in. The other thing Eve did was add on to the command of God when she said, "and you must not touch it or you will surely die" (Genesis 3:3). God never said not to touch the tree; He only said not to eat from the tree. Satan had managed to involve her in a game of semantics. Do not get into a conversation with Satan. When we entertain Satan, we often walk away with far more than our original sin problem. He is the author of confusion and clouds our thinking. He can distort the truth so we can't tell left from right.

Don't Respond Based on Your Feelings

Feelings can lead us astray. They are fickle and change like the wind. However, we often do side with our feelings. Siding with our feelings can lead us to make reckless and unwise decisions. We can change the way we feel by changing the way we think. Feelings follow thoughts, not the other way around. We feel something because we thought about it first. We reflect on a remark made by a friend who asked why we were not at the party the other night. We think long and hard about what she said, analyzing, dissecting, and thinking about why we were not invited. Soon we have concluded that no one likes us, we never get invited anywhere, and we have no friends. We start to have strong feelings based on our conclusion. Our feelings are centered on what we are thinking. When we change our thoughts, we change our feelings. If we don't give much thought to the remark our friend made, chances are likely we would not have feelings of being left out. Just because we feel a certain way doesn't make the situation true. Women often create these feelings in their minds and end up with damaged emotions because of them. Since Jesus was fully human, He also had feelings and desires. Out of hunger, He felt the desire to eat the bread when tempted. Yet, He chose not to respond to His feelings; rather, He responded based on the truth.

When confronted with a compromising situation, we should never respond based on our feelings. Make a decision to have a "cool down" period when feeling emotional, such as after an argument or disagreement with your husband. Choose not to respond to emails, texts, or social media for three days during that time. It is much wiser to calmly say a few chosen words later. We may regret and can never take back words rattled off in the heat of the moment. Arguments with our husbands will most likely be resolved, and our emotions will subside. We will be grateful we protected our emotional purity even when we felt emotional. We can often be irrational in the moment, so think about these decisions before the compromise arises.

Sometimes our feelings are so strong that we can't shake off the loneliness, anger, desire, guilt, or other feelings we may be dealing with. We need to go back to the truth of God's Word and mediate on it. When we change our thoughts, eventually our feelings will follow. If we pour energy and time into our feelings, they will only grow stronger and become more irrational. If we shift our thoughts to Scripture, prayer, and the truth of God's word, our thoughts will change our feelings. Some of us have had a long history of destructive thought patterns, so the feelings may not follow right away. This is similar to a person trying to lose weight. All the pounds will not be shed in the first week. It took years for the pounds to add up, and it will take weeks or months for them to come off. Slowly, the pounds slip away with exercise and proper diet. Similarly, old patterns in our thought lives do not go away instantly. They require work and diligence on our parts. The truth of God's Word is always true and will always guide us correctly. The feelings will slowly disappear as we align our thoughts to the truth of God's Word. This is important, because doing the right thing doesn't necessarily feel good. Sometimes, loving our husbands or staying committed to our marriages during a rough time doesn't feel good. We are called to be women who honor God because of His truth and not because of our feelings. Remember, feelings follow thoughts.

Prayer

Prayer sways the very heart of God. Prayer moves us to tell God our burdens, struggles, pains, deepest insecurities, guilt, and shame. The purpose of prayer is not for God to know all our concerns, because He is omniscient (all-knowing) and knows them already. The purpose is to intimately develop our relationship with Him and to be conformed into His image. The more we are conformed into His likeness, the less we will want to be like our old selves. Our fleshly desires fade as we get to know His character and attributes. We encounter His holiness as we experience Him and learn about our sin problem. The more we experience His holiness, the more we will want to run from our sin. If we are not moved to get down on our knees and pray over our sin, then everything else will be done in vain. Running from our sin is not enough. We must pray over it as well.

A woman confided in a friend that she was planning on divorcing her husband and was asking for prayer and support for her decision. The friend looked at the woman and said, "I don't need to pray about it. I know what God says about divorce, and you shouldn't divorce your husband." This godly lady did not need to seek God about the matter because she already knew where God stood on divorce. She knew God's

Word and wasn't afraid to speak the truth to her friend. While prayer is scriptural and we are called to pray continually, some things do not call for prayer because we already know what God says about them. Our prayers should be focused on seeking God's wisdom for the particular situation instead. If you are praying about something that is clear in Scripture, you may be asking for something that is contrary to the nature of God. God cannot and will not contradict His Word. If you are praying about whether to leave your husband, God is clear about this in Scripture. If you are praying about whether to connect with a man other than your husband, Scripture is clear. If you are praying about whether to join friends for an evening that contains a theme around adultery, Scripture is clear. God has already addressed these in His Word.

A powerful tool against the Enemy is combining prayer and Scripture. Prayer is our lifeline to God. Since His Word is alive and active, putting the two together is like dynamite when thrown in the face of Satan. One of the ingredients in dynamite is nitroglycerin. Interestingly enough, nitroglycerin is the main drug used to treat heart conditions and to prevent heart attacks. Nitroglycerin acts as a vasodilator, opening up clogged arteries so oxygen can get to the heart. Nitroglycerin in dynamite is highly explosive when combined with a few other simple ingredients. The same chemical used in warfare is used to clear the path to the heart. We need to apply the same principle in protecting our hearts and minds. The Enemy has declared war against us, and we must fight with weapons of supernatural power. Prayer and Scripture are like dynamite and explosive to the Enemy's tactics. They pave the way to allow our hearts to hear God's truth rather than Satan's lies. Choose Scripture verses. Insert your name in them, and pray them over yourself. Praying Scripture is a mighty and powerful weapon we have to fight with.

Guard against Triggers

We have identified several triggers (roller coaster moments) in the last chapter. Now we must determine which ones are our weaknesses. Maybe it is just one, two, or a combination of several. For instance, watching a certain television show when feeling lonely may not be a good combination. It's similar to surrounding ourselves with only chocolate when depressed. If our menstrual cycle causes us vulnerability, we should track our cycle. If struggles with our husbands make us vulnerable, it's probably wise to avoid connecting on social media during those struggles. If loneliness is our trigger, then we should try to avoid entertainment that highlights what we long for. Perhaps it is a friendship we know isn't healthy and we need to get away from. We should be in prayer, asking God to give us strength to fight off the temptation that is specific to us. Tell Him your struggle in this area. Tell Him what a temptation it is for you. He already knows, yet He wants and desires to help you. God wants to set us free from any sin that hinders us.

If our weakness is social media in general, then we may need to eliminate it altogether. Some of us might argue we can't live without our computers or cell phones. At one point, we all were without them and were fine. At least put up some safeguards around those items. Put a block on certain websites or close down a blog. Have your husband or a trusted friend check your cell phone frequently. Choose a package with your cable or satellite provider to eliminate the channels that may be a source of temptation. Install a password system on your television to block out compromising shows. Personally, I have discovered that doing without television is not as hard as it seems. I would turn to it in the evenings to relax when my kids were in bed. While trying to relax, garbage was sinking into my heart and my mind. The more garbage that came, the harder I had to work to get rid of it. Relaxing turned into work for me, and its purpose was self-defeating. I realize some of these boundaries seem extreme, but we all know what recommendation a financial advisor would give for people who have out-of-control spending and outrageous debt. Sin calls for extreme measures. God does not take sin lightly, and neither should we.

When something has become a source of temptation for us, it will most likely be a source of temptation again. Satan tends to use the same bait over and over. When we have bitten his bait once, he is hoping we will bite again. He usually doesn't change the bait until it stops working for us. He may then bring it again in the form of a different temptation.

Guarding our hearts is a daily task. The more we practice, the more effective and intentional we become. I have learned some valuable truths from the game of golf, which my boys play. My husband is very diligent in taking them to practice, and I often go watch them in tournaments or at practice. My husband tells them all the time that "practice makes permanent." The habits they create at practice will eventually become what they do in tournaments. Golf is all about purposeful routine and form. The form they practice will be the same form used during play. They cannot realistically expect to practice one way and then perform another way during a tournament. The habits we create during our spiritual "practice times" will prepare us in the same way when we are called to the frontlines of battle. The daily truths that we spend time meditating on will be the same ones that come to the forefront of our minds when we encounter temptations. If we fill our minds with impurity, we cannot expect Scripture to pop into our minds when we are in a fight with our husbands. If we read inappropriate novels, we cannot expect pure and pleasing thoughts when we are in a compromising situation.

When my boys first started golfing, they loved to go to the driving range and drive the really long shots. Their drives were impressive and often received attention and praise from others practicing. But as they started playing in tournaments, they quickly realized that the tee shot with the driver wasn't the only thing that counted. Sure, it was important, but they usually only hit the driver seven times in a nine-hole round. It was the other clubs that were used far more frequently, especially the putter, that really made the difference. The putter determined how they finished the game and required much more use. It required great skill. It required having the right line, hitting with just the right amount of speed, and learning to read which way the green breaks. The only way to learn was through practice. Now, practicing with the putter isn't nearly as fun or exciting as practicing with the driver. Not much glory or praise is given to the mundane small strokes taken over and over again on the putting green. The payoffs didn't come for my boys until the tournaments, but when they came, they were huge. They were often the difference between winning and losing. The daily choices we make add up in our lives as well. The small and routine things that seem so boring and often go unnoticed are very important. Memorizing small bits of Scripture adds up in the long run. The daily decisions we make to protect our emotional purity matter in the end. Do not underestimate the small decisions you make. Like golf, it is the small things that add up to the big thing.

Accountability

We should also become accountable to someone. That someone should be a trusted, godly girlfriend. Notice I said girlfriend—not a man but a woman. Perhaps you are new to your area and don't have a close friendship with anyone yet. Ask at your church for the name of a godly woman who would be willing to meet. A good resource would be the women's ministry director at your church. If your church doesn't have that position, check with the pastor's wife for suggestions of some names. Also, pray that God would provide someone specifically to minister to you.

There are many benefits to sharing our struggles with a friend. The most obvious is accountability. When we share our weaknesses, we are more likely to be kept accountable. If our weakness is our thought lives or social media, we should give permission to our accountability partners to ask about these things. We need to let these accountability partners invade our personal space, and we should not get angry when they do. They are not the enemy; our sin is the enemy. We should meet with our accountability partners on a regular basis to talk, pray, and memorize Scripture. James 5:16 tells us "to confess our sins to each other and pray for each other so that you may be healed." We need to be willing to let them see us for who we are—sinners in desperate need of Jesus. Transparency brings a new level of intimacy to the relationship.

One of the amazing things Jesus does is to bring beauty from our struggles. He uses us to affect other women who share the same struggle or are in similar circumstances. We may even be the difference as to whether they fight for their marriages or not. Do not underestimate what God can do with a transformed life. Psalm 51:17 says, "The sacrifices of God are a broken spirit, a broken and contrite heart." He uses broken people to influence those who are in desperate need for Jesus.

Chapter 11

Love Him for the Worst

Let the wicked forsake their ways and the unrighteous their thoughts. Let them turn to the Lord, and he will have mercy on them, and to our God, for he will freely pardon.

—Isaiah 55:7

If you are struggling with any form of pornography, a fantasy life, a relationship with another man, or just emotional satisfaction from movies, please know that there is hope and healing for you. It is not the end. To a repentant heart, Jesus always offers forgiveness, and only He has the power to provide the same forgiveness from your spouse. Remember, "If we confess our sins, He is faithful and just and will forgive us from our sins and purify us from all unrighteousness" (1 John 1:9).

This is a battle. The Enemy is waging war against our minds. We must admit our sin and seek forgiveness from God and our husbands. We must first repent of our sin to God. He is faithful to forgive us when we cry out to Him. There is great victory in exposing our sin to the light. Satan wants us to live in the darkness of our sin. He wants us to be paralyzed with fear. He makes us believe it would be better to live in shame and guilt than to expose our sins. He fills our minds with doubt, leading us to believe we are the only ones struggling. I can say with great confidence we are not the only ones.

We must also confess our sin to our husbands. This may not be easy, because there could be a variety of situations at play. First, your husband may already be aware of it, especially if it is something that has taken your sex life to a whole new level. He may even encourage you to keep up the sin if he is reaping rewards from it. You need to trust God through this and believe that He will honor your marriage if you honor Him. Do not limit God. He is not likely to bless you with a great sex life if you are in sin. We are called to be obedient to God's word. The other possibility is your husband may have no idea about your struggles. Confessing your sin to him may come as a complete surprise. He may be saddened or hurt to know his heightened sex life wasn't because of him. You need to be completely honest with him. Affirm your love for him and understand that healing may take some time, depending on the severity of the situation. If it is a situation involving a physical or emotional relationship with another man, please seek out professional counseling for the two of you.

Confessing our sin to our husbands also opens the door for communication. We have the opportunity to discuss what is important to us and what we need from them. This is not about finger pointing at husbands. It could be that that they are wonderfully attentive and doting husbands, and it is simply our sin at play. Or it could be a real wakeup signal to them that something is not right in our marriages and that our husbands might be part of the problem. They may see that we need more time and attention than they are providing us with. Perhaps this might be an opportunity to join a couples group or read a book together to strengthen our marriages. Know that God uses "all things for the good of those who love Him" (Romans 8:28). He can use the mistakes we make and the messes we create. Pray that God will use our circumstances to grow our marriages through Him.

If you are feeling neglected by your husband, first consider if you could be neglecting your husband as well. It is very easy to point the finger, but sometimes the finger needs to point back at us. Our husbands' needs are very different from ours. If we have been neglecting them, then our husbands might just be reacting out of their own hurt and pain. We all know what most husbands need and want from us. I said most—not all. We should use this as an opportunity to show them love and be more attentive to their needs. Even though we might not be feeling their love, the best way to receive love is to show love first. This is not easy to do if we feel neglected. Loving our husbands first can only come from the supernatural love of Jesus. Marriage is a cycle of needs—our husbands' needs and our needs. It only takes one to interrupt the flow. God wants us to step forward and meet their needs despite our own pain. Remember, we can only change ourselves. Love is a choice. If you are struggling to love your husband, ask God to change your desire to love him and to help you meet his needs unconditionally.

When our husbands know our weaknesses and struggles, this strengthens our marriages and provides marital accountability. This calls us to a higher standard, so we will be less likely to fall into the same traps again. This also demonstrates vulnerability to our husbands. Vulnerability is the one of the greatest building blocks to intimacy. Weaknesses unite and bring people closer together. The world screams at us to have inner strength. The world wants us to be strong, confident, and independent women. But Jesus says just the opposite. It is when we are weak that we are strong. It is through weaknesses that relationships are built, bonded, and sealed. When someone knows our greatest weaknesses but loves and accepts us anyway, our relationships are strengthened. It is freeing to know that no matter how badly we mess up, someone will still love us.

Love Him While He Is a Sinner

While we want unconditional love and acceptance from our husbands despite our struggles, we also need to communicate the same to them. When we took our marriage vows, we committed to love one another in sickness or health, for richer or poorer, or for better or for worse. These are the moments we said we would love our husbands. It is easy to love our husbands for the best. It is much harder to love them for the worst. A friend's husband got into an accident, and he was unable to do much for himself because of his injuries. He turned to his wife and asked her if she would wipe his bottom for him if he needed it. That's definitely "for worse." Her "for worse" marriage vow was summed up in that question. Our "for worse" could be different. It could be when our husbands come home from work and are not up for a conversation. It might be when they take an interest in spending more time with their buddies than with us. It may be when they are lured into pornography. Worse yet, it could involve an affair with a coworker, client, friend, or acquaintance. That is "for worse." Yet, we vowed we would love them. We committed to it before our husbands, families, friends, and God. This is not meant to excuse any of the above behavior from our husbands. However, we cannot be women who give up on our men because they mess up.

Loving our husbands through other worsts is far easier than through affairs. Some of us are dealing with some pretty heavy things in our marriages. Years of deep wounds and resentment have piled up. Hurt that seems unbearable and beyond repair floods some of our minds. While we cannot make light of this pain, we need to point ourselves to Jesus as the great healer, Jehovah Rapha. Our husbands may have done some pretty bad things, but none of us would abandon our children because of a foolish decision. Most of us would say that there is nothing our children could do that would make us stop loving them. Somehow, some of us have justified not forgiving our husbands. However, forgiving our children knows no limit. We have not been given the authority to draw a line to say some things are worthy of forgiveness while others are not when it comes to our husbands. When we choose not to forgive our husbands, our pride is saying they are not worthy of our forgiveness. God has not appointed us the judge to determine which sin is worthy of forgiveness and which is not. He is the great Judge, and He commands us to forgive. We cannot be women who say that our love and forgiveness stop at a certain point. We cannot be women who say some things are worthy of forgiveness while other things are not. Pride has no place in marriages.

We must be women who give our husbands the same unconditional love that we offer our children. We need to build that same acceptance and love into our marriages. We need to demonstrate that no matter how badly our spouses mess up, we will still love and accept them. There is hope and healing, even in the grimmest of circumstances. God hates divorce, and He is the author of forgiveness. I have witnessed Him mend and heal marriages that seemed completely hopeless. God is capable. He is willing to heal, because where there is forgiveness, there is always hope. Jesus called us to be women who forgive abundantly, because this is how He forgives us.

God has taught me a valuable lesson in forgiveness through my daughter. When she makes a mistake, she is quick to apologize and ask for forgiveness. After repeatedly apologizing for the same mistake, I responded very hastily once when she came to apologize. I told her that I was tired of hearing the words "I'm sorry" and wanted to see a change in her behavior. I felt the piercing arrows of conviction from God asking me, "How many times have you come to Me with the same sin over and over again?" I realized how wrong my words were and that I needed to forgive her without end. I was communicating to her that my forgiveness was dependent on her behavior, which is completely the opposite of what Christ says. He says, "Come to Me and I will change you" rather than "Change and then come to Me." He accepts us as we are and opens the floodgates of forgiveness and mercy. Romans 5:8 says, "While we were still sinners, Christ died for us." God loves us while we are still sinners, and that is how we must love our husbands.

The apostle Paul wrote the following about marriage: "To the married I give this command (not I, but the Lord): A wife must not separate from her husband. But if she does, she must remain unmarried or else be reconciled to her husband. And a husband must not divorce his wife" (1 Corinthians 7:10–11). Our marriages are symbolic of Christ's relationship with the church. Jesus is the head or husband of the church, which is His bride (Ephesians 5). Christ cares for His church lovingly and has promised to never abandon her. The two are united in a covenant relationship, which is an agreement made by God with His people. Our marriages are covenant relationships between God and us. God's Word is clear that the marriage covenant should not be broken. Scripture is full of covenants made by God to His people, and He fulfilled every one of them. He made a covenant with Noah never to flood the earth again and with Abraham to be the father of many nations. When God made a covenant to Moses to deliver the Israelites from slavery in Egypt, He didn't abandon them at the Red Sea or walk away when they had no food. He provided for them along the journey and delivered them to the Promised Land. He fulfilled His promise of deliverance completely and wholeheartedly. God always keeps His promises. He does nothing halfway, and He calls us to be women who do the same with our marriage covenants. We will never be geared toward holiness if we declare our love for Christ and denounce our love for our husbands in the same breath.

If you are considering leaving your husband, I urge you to stop and get some godly counsel before you proceed any further. To some who may already be divorced, there is always the possibility of reconciliation with your spouse. To those for whom there is not that possibility, there is healing. Perhaps there may be a ministry opportunity for you to influence other women and spare them the heartache and hardship that divorce brings. Friends, we do not have the right to divorce our husbands. I have witnessed countless women leave marriages because of their husband's infidelity, sickness, or mental illness. These are not sufficient reasons for divorce. With God, no reason is sufficient.

I want to share a story with you that is close to my heart. It is about a sister in Christ who has taught me much about marriage. Her husband and she share thirty-five years of marriage together. There is a lifetime of joy mixed in with hurt and pain, as with any marriage. A few years ago, he left her. He has not divorced her for various reasons. Although they live apart, they are still legally married. She does not want a divorce and is fighting for her marriage. He has lost money and has had affairs during this separation. Yet, she continues on with life through the hurt and pain. She is often alone during holidays and special days. Anniversaries are a painful reminder of the life she once shared with him. Here is where the story gets interesting. She doesn't just sit at home having a big pity party, although you would think she has every reason in the world to do so. She leads a Bible study and ministers to other women. She opens her empty home to those needing a temporary place to stay. She is actively involved in her church and financially sponsors several children around the world. She sponsored one through his entire dental school training. She is always willing to give and continually prays about where God might use her next. She gets up every morning, puts on her makeup, and fixes her hair because today could be the day her husband walks through the door. Today could be the day she has prayed for, wept over, and clung to with hope. She prays and cries out Scripture over her husband every morning and night. She prays God would change his heart. She prays God would do such a mighty work in his life that there would be no question it was from Him. She knows that when God changes his heart, he will be a new man from the inside out. Yes, she has hard, lonely, and extremely painful days. Yet she continues to trust her Creator in faith that He has called her to stand for her marriage. She realizes she is swimming upstream, even in the Christian world, where she is told it is acceptable to divorce because of his infidelity. God has called her to love her husband through his rejection of her. He has called her to be a living example to the women around her experiencing their own marital crises. If you asked her, she would tell you that she is only doing what God has commanded her to do, which is to stand firmly by her covenant husband.

You may think my friend is an extraordinary woman. While there is no doubt she is pretty special, she is doing something that all of us can choose to do if we find ourselves in similar circumstances. She is simply doing what God has commanded. She is standing by her marriage vows. In the culture we live in, we deem this spectacular. In God's eyes, it is simply obedience. This should be the norm among Christians, not the amazing and incredible story we hear every now and then. She is standing by her husband the same way Christ has stood by her. She is willing to forgive him just as Christ forgave her. She has taught me a lot about the sanctity of marriage. When we view marriage through God's eyes, it changes everything.

Chapter 12

Stake Your Marriage

Therefore, holy brothers and sisters, who share in the heavenly calling, fix your thoughts on Jesus, whom we acknowledge as our apostle and high priest.
—Hebrews 3:1

My Husband Is Not My Prince

I know some of you are shocked to learn your husband is actually not Prince Charming. My husband teases me that instead of marrying Prince Charming, I ended up with Prince Alarming. For some of you, this isn't funny. You may be suffering and hurting in a marriage where there isn't the fulfillment you expected. You are in a marriage where you long and desire for more than your husband is giving. The love, romance, tenderness, or communication that you intensely desire just isn't there. Sometimes we can pray about our needs, communicate them to our husbands, and there will still be no change. We then need to come to a place of acceptance. I am not suggesting that this is your lot in life so you should just deal with it. The acceptance I am speaking about is recognizing that Jesus knows exactly what you need, and for some reason He is having you endure your current circumstance. As Scripture teaches, "Each person should live as a believer in whatever situation the Lord has assigned to them" (1 Corinthians 7:17). Jesus knows you are hurting. He cries with you over your pain. He has brought you to this place, and you must trust Him through it. You can rest solely in the fact that He is in control and is working on your behalf. Yes, you will wish, hope, dream, and pray that one day things will change. But for now, you must trust God. Trusting God brings us to a place of inner peace that only He can provide. It brings us to a place of acceptance of our circumstances, even if they have never changed.

Another thing we must do is praise God through our pain. We often associate praise with victories and success in our lives. God is worthy of praise regardless of our circumstances, whether difficult or easy. He deserves praise and honor based on who He is and not based on our circumstances. He is worthy of praise simply because He is God. Unless we learn to give Him praise through our difficulties, our faith will be hindered because our love for Him will be conditional. If we only love God when He is good to us, we are only loving Him because of what He can do for us rather than for who He is. Daniel and David praised God through fear of death and persecution. Even Joseph, who was sold into slavery, falsely accused, and thrown in prison, recognized God was worthy of praise despite his circumstances. When we can praise God through our pain, the victories will taste much sweeter.

Stake Your Marriage

We need to be women who claim our marriages for Christ regardless of whether a marital struggle exists. If you are struggling in your marriage, take some time and pray for God to show you areas in your life where you may have allowed sin to creep in. Think about the shows you watch, the books you read, the websites you visit, and the thoughts you think when you are alone. Think about where you invest most of your time. Not all marital struggles are the result of our sin, but often they can be. Ask God to reveal any areas you might not be aware of. Any sin you may have to give up is worth the price for the sake of your marriage.

Even if things are fine in our marriages, we still need to claim our marriages for Christ. Claiming our marriages means taking ownership of what is rightly ours. The day we said "I do," our marriages became ours, and we need to boldly stake that truth. Suppose the bank contacted us stating that there was some confusion over our accounts and someone else was claiming our accounts as theirs. We would never sit back and let them rob what we have labored so hard to earn. We would fight, and we would fight hard. We would dig up papers, records, and account slips to claim what was rightfully ours. Our marriages and our husbands are ours. We need to claim this truth daily because someone is trying to rob us of our marriage. Someone is trying to steal what we have worked for and invested in. We need to mark and stake our territory. Sister, put your stake in your husband (not literally!), because he belongs to you!

The Perfect Prince

There is wonderful news for those struggling with the fact that their husbands are not Prince Charming. We all have a Prince Charming. This Prince Charming is someone our husband was never intended to be. Jesus is our Prince Charming because He is perfect. He is even referred to in Scripture as the "Prince of Peace." He rescues us, pursues us relentlessly, woos us gently, and speaks kindly to us. He listens attentively and always has time for us. He holds us in our grief and pain and is our ultimate comforter. Nothing we say will make Him turn His back on us or walk away. He will never tell us there is someone prettier, younger, or with a better body than ours. He always responds with mercy, grace, and forgiveness. No mess of ours is too great or too awful. He gently picks us up and places us on our feet and sets us back on solid ground. We are His, and He will never let us go. Never. Isaiah 54:5 says, "For the Maker is your husband—the Lord Almighty is his name—the Holy One of Israel is your Redeemer; He is called the God of all the earth." Scripture says God is ultimately our husband no matter what our relationship is with our earthly husband. Jesus is the perfect man for us.

Several years ago our family moved from South Florida to Georgia. I immediately fell in love with the trees, the change of seasons, and the cooler weather. When people learned we had moved from Florida, they were shocked we would ever leave. After all, Florida has beaches, the ocean, and regular sunshine. I was equally shocked to discover Georgia residents drove many hours just to vacation at the beach. I grew up with the beach in my backyard, and when you have it in your backyard, you don't need to go vacationing at the beach. To me, the beach was the beach. Sure, it was neat, but it had become nothing special because I saw it practically every day of my life while growing up. The sense of wonder and amazement along with its beauty just faded into the background. I had forgotten how beautiful the clear blue sky was, how sparkling and warm the water felt, and how sweet the salty air smelled. I had forgotten because it was there all the time. When I go back to visit and see the beach, I see things I completely took for granted.

Some of us know Jesus but have lost our awe and wonder of Him. We may have grown up in the church and been saved at a young age, but we live as if He is nothing special to us anymore. He has just faded into the background of everyday life. We sometimes forget what it is like to have Jesus as our healer, counselor, best friend, and husband. We have forgotten that we don't have to be lonely, depressed, anxious, or fearful. We have access to the Creator of the universe, and all we have to do is call out to Him. Jesus does not want to be just another part of our lives. He wants to be our life. He wants to be our everything and for us to be everything through Him. Acts 17:28 says, "For in Him, we live, and move, and have our being."

Some of you have never let Jesus be your prince. You may love Him, but if your primary source of fulfillment is the man in your life, you have probably been sorely disappointed. You may be having an affair. You may be experiencing all the wonderful feelings your husband never gave you, but it is short-lived. This man will let you down as well. You may be involved in a texting relationship. Eventually the sweet words will come to an end. The emotional satisfaction from a book or movie will leave you empty. All of these sources will never offer you the kind of love only Jesus gives. Even if you have the greatest husband in the world, he will let you down as well. You will come to a point during the course of your marriage when you realize your happiness and joy should not and does not come from your husband. He cannot realistically make you happy, and he shouldn't have to try. Coming to this realization sooner rather than later will save you much grief. But when it does come, there is such freedom, contentment, and peace. Whether your earthly husband is a great man who meets your needs, or whether he never meets any of your needs, turn to Jesus. He will meet every longing in your heart. When we turn to Jesus as our source of fulfillment, we take our husbands off the pedestal and relieve them of unrealistic expectations. This frees our men to be who they are with all their flaws. It frees us to love and accept them without all of those expectations. When we turn to Jesus, there is freedom for us, our husbands, and our marriages.

Stake Your Eternity

Just as we need to stake our marriages, we also need to stake our eternities. We can stake our eternities by claiming the free gift of eternal life offered to us by God. As Scripture says, "He himself bore our sins, in his body on the cross, so that we might die to sins and live for righteousness; by his wounds you have been healed" (1 Peter 2:24). Jesus went to the cross for us because our sin is so great, and it was the only way restitution could be made. He took the penalty for our sins and endured the shame, suffering, and pain. He chose to suffer so we wouldn't have to. It is not enough to simply believe in God. The Bible says even the demons believe God exists. He loves us so much that He wants more. He wants us to hand over our lives to Him. He wants to be in control of our lives. Acknowledge you have sinned, made a mess of things, and can't do life on your own. Ask Him to forgive you and for Him to be in control. Once you do, you become an intimate friend of Jesus and can go to Him in prayer anytime you want or need. God will give you the Holy Spirit to guide, convict, and provide assurance that you belong to Him. Nobody can ever take that away from you. You have also been promised that you will spend eternity with Him when you die. Romans 10:9 says, "If you confess with your mouth, 'Jesus is Lord,' and believe in your heart that God raised him from the dead, you will be saved." By giving your life to Jesus, you claim the free gift of eternal life and put your stake in eternity. If you made this decision, are thinking about making it, or have questions about it, please talk to someone in a Christian church. Please make sure that the Word of God (the Bible) is taught there and that Jesus is proclaimed as the only way to receive God's salvation.

Chapter 13

Women on a Rescue Mission

*Therefore if you have any encouragement from being
united with Christ, if any comfort from his love, if
any common sharing in the Spirit, if any tenderness
and compassion, then make my joy complete by being
like-minded, having the same love, being one in spirit
and mind.*

—*Philippians 2:1–2*

Many of us may not be caught in sinful emotional struggles,
but chances are we know someone who is. It may even be a
good friend. So what should we do if we know a friend is in
sin? Most of us seem to do one of two things. First, we might
turn our back to it and act as if it isn't really there. We do this
for the same reason we turn our heads when we see a homeless
person on the street corner. Or when we hear about children
dying of hunger in another country, we sometimes tune it
out by changing the channel. Deep down, we all know the
homeless man or the dying child didn't disappear just because
we turned our head. They are still there. They just aren't in
our realm of existence. For some strange reason, if we can't see
them, it makes us feel better about ourselves because it excuses
their need in our minds. This is a selfish approach because our

focus shifts from the poor and the hungry to ourselves. There is a great example of this in the Bible with the story of the Good Samaritan in Luke 10. A man is robbed and left for dead on the side of road. Two separate travelers pass by him and do nothing to help him. Finally, a third traveler sees him and has mercy on him. He bandages his wounds and takes him to an inn, paying the bill. It was easier for the first two travelers to simply ignore the injured man.

Another reason people turn their backs to sin is because of image. We are overly concerned with how we will be perceived by others if we are seen with "the sinner." This approach points to an elevated view of oneself. We are all sinners, and no one is above a particular sin or better than another person.

The second thing people tend to do when they witness sin is to talk incessantly about it to others. We may talk about it to our neighbors or our girlfriends. We may even share it at our Bible study group as a "prayer request." Perhaps part of the reason we talk about it is to gossip or use it as a conversation piece. In these situations, if we haven't confronted the sinner, we certainly have no right sharing it with others. Another reason we gossip is because it makes us feel better about ourselves. We think it makes us look better because it elevates us to a category different from the sinner. Our egos get puffed up with self-righteousness. It also puts us in position as "the one who knows it all" or "the first one to get the story." We use someone else's struggle for our own personal gain. This too is a very selfish approach since the focus is shifted to us once again.

These are often our approaches when we witness sin. All of them are selfish approaches, whether we keep our distance or gossip. Even though we know what we witness is wrong, we often do nothing and say nothing to help. We convince ourselves with self-justifying thoughts, such as *It's none of my business* or *I don't want to get involved.* But it is our business. James 4:17 says, "If anyone, then, knows the good they ought to do and doesn't do it, it is sin for them." Scripture says if we know the right thing to do and do not do it, we sin. God gives us very clear directions in Scripture that we are to deal with sin, and He gives us directions on how to handle it.

Rescue

God sent His Son into the world on the greatest rescue mission known to man. Jesus was born, crucified, and died to ultimately rescue us from our sin. God often puts us in the paths of others for rescue missions as well. While we can never erase someone's sin, we can greatly influence and encourage others who may be headed for destruction. God may even use us to help save someone. James 5:19–20 says, "My brothers and sisters, if one of you should wander from the truth and someone should bring that person back, remember this: whoever turns a sinner from the error of their way saves them from death and cover over a multitude of sins." When someone is standing in the middle of a busy highway, we can yell and scream at the person, but the best intervention is to take action by running out and pulling the person to safety. It takes boldness and courage, and it requires some effort. Imagine the same effort with a friend caught in a web of sin. Proverbs 24:11 says, "Rescue those being led away to death; hold back those staggering toward slaughter." Rescue is an action verb, which means it requires physical action on our parts. A conversation to warn a friend of the danger she is in may be all it takes. If it takes more, we need to be willing to do more. If telling her isn't enough, we cannot wipe our hands clean and move on with life. We cannot move on thinking, *I warned her, so my job is done.*

Often, our interventions will require much more than having just a conversation. They will require our time and energy. They will mean exhausting our prayer lives and possibly fasting on behalf of our friends. It will mean getting involved in their lives, and getting our physical and emotional hands dirty and messy. This is hard and difficult because we like clean Christianity. On the contrary, nothing about Christianity is clean. It is filled with dirty, filthy, sin-ridden people in desperate need of Jesus. But Jesus takes the dirty, broken sinners, and He uses them mightily. Scripture is full of people who committed murder, adultery, and prostitution. God rescued them for His purpose and His glory, ultimately bringing the Savior through their bloodline.

Jesus told several parables about people who went on rescue missions including a shepherd who lost his sheep, a woman who lost a silver coin, and a father who lost his son to wild living (Luke 15). The shepherd and the woman went to great lengths to find their lost treasures. The father whose son was lost was filled with love and compassion and ran out to greet him when he saw him returning home. Jesus went all the way on His rescue mission, since He died for us. He did it because we are worth it. Other people are worth it too. They are worth it to Jesus, and they should be worth it to us. We need to be women willing to rescue because we were once rescued. We need to be willing to rescue even if it means getting dirty and messy along the way.

Forgiveness

One of the fundamentals of the Christian faith is forgiveness. We are commanded to forgive because we too have been forgiven. Luke 17:3 says, "If your brother sins, rebuke him and if he repents, forgive him. If he sins against you seven times a day and seven times comes back to you and says 'I repent,' forgive him." Jesus says we are to acknowledge the sin and confront our friends lovingly. We should pray God gives us the right hearts without judgment or condemnation—hearts that are kind, gentle, and loving. There is no shame in forgiveness. Shame is hurtful, vengeful, and wrong. If we want to be heard, we must have the right spirit. Our step then is to forgive the sinner.

Proverbs 17:17 says, "A friend loves at all times, and a brother is born for a time of adversity." Scripture doesn't provide exceptions to forgiveness, because it isn't dependent on the measure of sin. Just as with our spouses, we are not to decide which sins are worthy of forgiveness and which are not. Forgiveness is one-size-fits-all; it covers everything. Loving a friend through forgiveness may be hard, sticky, and messy. Often it may be difficult if we have been hurt or betrayed in the process. But this is what true love is, to forgive one another even in the most difficult circumstances. Proverbs 27:6 says, "Wounds from a friend can be trusted, but an enemy multiplies kisses." We are also commanded to forgive repeatedly. Forgiving over and over demonstrates how Jesus forgives us. When we go to Jesus with the same junk day after day, He forgives without question or hesitation. He doesn't make us relive it or pay for it. He doesn't require us to say sorry a million times, and He doesn't give us a guilt trip. He just forgives. Where there is sorrow and repentance, there should always be forgiveness. We will not accurately portray the gospel to anyone without godly forgiveness. Through forgiveness, we demonstrate love to others, pointing them to Christ.

Often, Christians will bail on a friend who shows no repentance and remorse over her sin. Bailing on an unrepentant friend is conditional love. We love her as long as she operates under a certain set of rules or conditions. This is not the response Jesus commands of us. Romans 5:8 says, "But God demonstrates his own love for us in this: While we were still sinners, Christ died for us." The gospel rests on grace, which God freely offered us while we were still in sin. He wants us to offer to others the same forgiveness and love that He has given us. When we do, we love unconditionally because of grace, not because of the condition of our friends' hearts.

Scripture says, "If anyone does not obey our instructions in this letter, take special note of him. Do not associate with him, in order that he may feel ashamed. Yet, do not regard him as an enemy, but warn him as a brother" (2 Thessalonians 3:14). The word *associate* comes from the Greek word "to mix together with."[7] Associate is to mix with someone's lifestyle, to live life the way he or she does. We are clearly commanded against this since we are told to be "in the world, not of the world." We can, however, be a part of an unrepentant friend's life without adopting her standards. There is a big difference between living someone's lifestyle and ministering to her. Most people stop at the word *ashamed* and do not read further in this Scripture reference. We are commanded to regard her as a sister, not as an enemy. Having lunch and keeping in touch with an unrepentant friend is loving her. Being concerned about her and offering to pray for her is what is commanded of us. Luke 7:34 describes Jesus as "a friend of sinners" because He hung out with tax collectors and prostitutes. Mark 2:17 says, "It is not the healthy who need a doctor, but the sick. I have not come to call the righteous but the sinners." After all, Jesus came for sinners, people like you and me in desperate need of Him. Enemies separate and isolate. Friends love unconditionally. The goal is restoration and to bring the unrepentant back into fellowship. It is the kindness of God that leads us to repentance. Our kindness will influence others to repentance as well.

Restoration

Our next step is to be an encourager in order to bring restoration. Listen to what Galatians 6:1 says: "Brothers and sisters, if someone is caught in a sin, you who live by the spirit should restore that person gently. But watch yourselves, or you also may be tempted." As women, we know how easy it is to drown in sorrow and guilt. We must rid ourselves of the attitude that leads us to say, "She got what she deserved." It is unnecessary and wrong to pile guilt and shame on someone. She needs a heart that gives no shame, doesn't heap on guilt, and lifts her spirits. God is fully capable of sorting out real and false guilt; He does not need our help. She needs a heart that grieves with her when she cries over past mistakes or any losses she might have suffered. We need to reach into this friend's pit and pull her out through prayer and Scripture. We need to stand beside her through the tough moments. She needs her reputation protected through the gossip and when others look with condemning eyes. We need to be her friend when the rest of the world bails.

Celebration

In all three of the parables Jesus told in Luke 15, there was great rejoicing. The shepherd, the woman, and the father celebrated because what was once lost was now found. The father threw his lost son a party in honor of his return. He had a celebration because his wayward son repented of his ways. Think of all the life moments we celebrate: milestone birthdays, anniversaries, and weddings. We throw elaborate and expensive events for nice but less than life-changing moments. We tend to overlook moments that define and change us. The moments and decisions that affect our eternities go unnoticed. Imagine attending a party in honor of a girlfriend's changed heart instead of a fortieth birthday party. Imagine gathering to celebrate a couple whose marriage has been saved and reconciled or an alcoholic who has remained sober. There are many ways we can celebrate a friend. We can write a note, take her out to dinner, or even give a small gift. More than anything, I believe, it is the attitude of our hearts toward her that makes the difference in celebration. It is the way we respond to and treat her. She needs a heart that loves and accepts her exactly the way she is. She needs a heart that unconditionally loves her, because that is how Jesus loves us. A changed heart and life is cause for great celebration because a sinner has been brought from death to life. Luke 15:10 says, "In the same way, I tell you, there is rejoicing in the presence of angels of God over one sinner who repents." In the same way the angels of God rejoice over just one sinner, we must be women who rejoice with others as well.

One of the greatest examples of a rescue mission in the Bible is the story of the adulterous woman in John 8:1–11. The Pharisees brought a woman caught in adultery to Jesus and asked Him if she should be stoned since it was what the law required. Picture the scene. They made this poor woman stand before a large gathering of people just after Jesus began to teach in the temple. They made a public spectacle of her with every condemning eye on her while she trembled in fear. They questioned Jesus about what to do with her. If they knew what the law said, they didn't need to ask. We, too, often ask questions or make comments about others when we know the answers. We do it in a selfish attempt to make ourselves known through another's crisis. Think of how many times we bring attention to someone or something just to prove we are "in the know."

Jesus then began to write on the ground with His finger. We don't know what He wrote, but we do know He wrote silently. Perhaps He was thinking and choosing His words carefully. Or maybe He was praying. His silence speaks volumes to us on how we should respond. Silence helps shape our thoughts and helps us carefully choose our words. It helps tame our emotions and control our tone of voice. It helps us avoid saying something we might regret later. Proverbs 10:19 says, "Sin is not ended by multiplying words, but the prudent hold their tongues." The wise woman shuts her mouth when emotions are flying in every direction. The wise woman remains silent to realign her focus on God and shape her response against the truth of His Word rather than on her feelings. This is difficult in a world where everyone wants to be heard and have the last word. But it is not how Jesus wants us to be. Jesus never screamed or yelled to be heard. He did just the opposite. He spoke the truth of God's Word when necessary and often responded with silence. Often silence is more powerful and effective than saying a word.

The Pharisees kept questioning Him. Jesus confidently stood up, turned to the angry crowd, and invited anyone without sin to cast the first stone. He then bent down for a second time to write on the ground. Slowly the stones began to drop. When only Jesus and the woman were left, He stood up and asked the woman if anyone had condemned her. When she replied, "No," He said, "Then I do not condemn you either; now go and leave your life of sin." This woman must have been shaking and crying, thinking she would be stoned to death because of her sin. In a matter of moments, the crowd that had once condemned her was gone. Imagine: she was then suddenly left alone with Jesus. Because of His grace and mercy, her life was changed forever both physically and spiritually. Jesus loved her. Because He loved her, He forgave her. No longer bound by the sin of her past, she was freed. Jesus rescued her while she was still in her sin. This is the reason why Jesus came, to rescue people.

Like Jesus, we need to be women who hate the sin but love the sinner. We need to be women on rescue missions. We need to be women who are not afraid to speak the truth lovingly to others when they are in sin. With our words, we will either condemn or forgive. With mercy and forgiving spirits, we too can offer freedom and healing to a fellow sister. We must be women who forgive and stand by our broken sisters, because we are no different. Even if we haven't committed the offense physically, most of us have committed it in our minds. We are all guilty. Emulating what Jesus did for us points to a beautiful picture of the gospel.

Emotional Stumbling Blocks

Most of us have not had physical affairs, but many of us have caused a man to stumble. Setting stumbling blocks is an intentional act meant to trip or make someone fall. It is similar to setting a small stone in someone's path. We know he won't see it, and we know he will trip, but we do it anyway. Most of us would never try to trip someone physically. Yet many of us do it all the time with the way we dress, with our words, or even with the way we act. Leading a man astray can be emotional; it is not just physical. Any personal relationship with a man besides our husband can be a potential stumbling block. Stumbling blocks can be physical, emotional, or media-based.

Causing a man to glance or notice us because of our low-cut tops or short skirts may make us feel pretty and desirable, but it may be at the expense of causing him to sin. Remember, men are visually attracted to women. Dressing a certain way because we know a man will be present sets up a stumbling block for him. Some of us dress nicer for other people than we do for our own husbands. Save the cute outfit for your own man, and perhaps he will notice you. It just might be the spark your marriage needs.

Our words can be a stumbling block for a man also. Offering choice words that lead him to hunger or lust is wrong. We should be very careful with words that a man could easily misinterpret. A good boundary is to not get into personal conversations with the opposite sex without our husbands present. The conversation does not have to be sexual to be wrong. Most of us would never engage in lengthy conversations with another man alone in a private room. We need to have the same standard with conversations on social media, cell phones, and emails.

Our conduct can cause a man to sin as well. Walking a certain way, sometimes the longer way, in order to catch another man's attention is wrong. Purposely brushing against him so he will notice us is wrong as well. We may be getting the attention we desire, but in doing so, we become a stumbling block for him. This is not what God desires from us. We are preying on a man's weakness, and this is not acceptable. This should be saved for our own husbands. We would never want other women to entice our husbands, and we should hold ourselves to the same standard. Listen to what Romans 14:13 says: "Therefore let us stop passing judgment on one another. Instead make up your mind not to put any stumbling block or obstacle in the way of a brother or sister." God takes stumbling blocks very seriously, because when we set them up, we cause another to sin. We become a hindrance in another's pursuit of holiness. Matthew 18:6 says, "If anyone causes one of these little ones—those who believe in me—to stumble, it would be better for them to have a large millstone hung around their neck and to be drowned in the depths of the sea." God will hold us accountable when we lead others astray.

Stealing Glances

Before a home is built on a lot, it is carefully measured and staked to ensure that everything is done according to code without infringing on our neighbors' properties. Stakes are put in at the corners of our lot where our boundary lines begin and end. Our marriages have boundary lines as well (a wife having one husband, keeping the marriage bed pure, and so on). We are not to infringe on someone else's marriage; nor is anyone else to infringe on ours. Do not take something that does not belong to you, including another woman's marriage. And don't let anyone else take yours. Often we may think as long as we don't take someone's marriage, we are in the clear. However, we may be stealing plenty of other things from another woman. It may be a conversation that rightfully belongs to her, or a glance from her husband at our revealing outfit. We can even rob her of time with her husband. Job 24:2 speaks of this: "There are those who move boundary stones; they pasture flocks they have stolen." We must keep our minds, thoughts, and emotions on our own flocks, where they rightfully belong.

We must be careful we do not set up stumbling blocks or steal things that do not belong to us. Whether our clothes, our words, or our conduct is to blame doesn't matter. It's not about our "right" to do something. It's about God's standard of holiness. We gave up our rights in order to pursue righteousness when we became followers of Christ. As the body of Christ, we are to spur one another on toward holiness. We are never to hinder it.

Chapter 14

Guarding the Hearts of the Next Generation

Fix these words of mine in your hearts and minds; tie them as symbols on your hands and bind them on your foreheads. Teach them to your children, talking about them when you sit at home and when you walk along the road, when you lie down and when you get up.
                                    —*Deuteronomy 11:18–19*

We teach our little girls how to be proper and polite. We paint their toenails and pierce their ears. We take them shopping for their first bras and have "the talk" with them when they are of age. We help them pick out dresses for the dance and eventually help them fill out college applications. Then we help them plan their weddings. We might be missing some very important things to teach them along their journeys to womanhood, though. These are things we wish someone had told us—things that will serve them well in their emotional lives and in their marriages. If we don't tell them, no one else will. They will be left to deal with their emotions, alone and confused.

One of Her Greatest Vulnerabilities Will Be Her Mind

Don't you wish someone had told you how emotionally vulnerable your mind would be? I know most of our mothers did the best they could when raising us. But let's face it: most of us came from a generation of mothers who said very little to us. It was a different time, and they only did what they knew how to do. We are in a different time, and a different approach is needed with our daughters. So not only do we need to tell our daughters about the dangers of premarital sex, we also need to explain the emotional vulnerability of their minds. We know how easy it is to have our minds taken captive.

When I was a young college student working a summer job, a few coworkers invited me over to look at pornographic pictures of men. I politely declined and sat awkwardly as they giggled and huddled together. To this day, I am thankful I did not look. My gratitude is not because I like to look at pictures of naked men, but because those images would have stuck in my mind permanently. No one had taught me it was wrong, but in my spirit I knew it was wrong. At the time, I had no idea how detrimental the effects could be. We need to tell our girls this. There will be coworkers, roommates, dorm leaders, and even friends who will invite them to do and see things their fragile minds are not meant to see and read. These things are damaging and carry over into their relationships and eventually into their marriages. Some of those images, thoughts, and words will never escape them. Just as the images of pornography can lure and seduce a young man into a lifelong struggle, the mind of a young woman can be lured into an emotional struggle.

Don't be fooled into thinking your little girl will never battle this. She will. She may be sweet, innocent, and pure, but because she is a woman, her emotional state is raw and vulnerable. Everywhere they turn, our daughters are facing these battles—and at a much younger age than we ever had to. We must warn our daughters of the dangers of certain shows that tug at a woman's emotions. We must warn them about the certain book on the bestseller list, and the invitations on social media. We must teach them to guard their minds and emotions by being careful what they see, read, and hear. We must demonstrate to them that we don't watch certain programs because of their potential influence on us. We must teach them how to guard their minds through Scripture and prayer. We must teach them how to run from emotional impurity just as they would from alcohol or drugs.

Purity Is Not Just Physical

It is interesting how we think of sexual purity as just physical. While growing up, I used to think that as long as I was sexually pure, that was good enough. It's not that I didn't care, but no one told me there was more to it. No one told me God wanted my mind protected just like my body. Don't let your daughter be deceived into thinking physical purity is enough. It is not. We need to teach our girls that purity also involves the heart and mind. God commands us to be emotionally pure as well as physically pure. He wants us to love Him with every part of our beings. Tell your daughter God desires her to give every aspect of her body and mind to Him. Tell her guarding her body with her boyfriend is important, but guarding her mind is equally important when she is with friends or alone. When she begins to view purity in its entirety, she will understand why she needs to protect her mind, since it affects every area of her life. She will honor God by protecting her emotional purity.

A Man's Role Is Not to Bring Her Fulfillment or Happiness

Many young women make vows on their blissful wedding days only to realize their handsome, charming, and smart husbands aren't what they thought they would be. Honestly, the whole Prince Charming fantasy is hyped up during childhood. I am not trying to spoil dreams or put a damper on romance, but consider the disappointment we set our little girls up for with this high expectation of marriage. A little girl grows up thinking her man will be perfect in stature and appearance. He will live in a castle because his father will be the king and will have unlimited amounts of money and resources. Then they will live happily ever after. Really? No disagreements? No dirty socks left on the floor or toilet seat left up? No grunting or snoring? Most girls outgrow this fairy tale romance, but many still enter marriage with the "happily ever after" notion and the thought that their men are perfect. They think their men will never hurt them, say unkind words to them, or fail to communicate with them. Let's tell them so they won't be shocked in marriage and wonder if they made a mistake. Let's warn our daughters that one day, their husbands might not communicate as much as they did when they were dating. They need to know it doesn't mean they don't love them, but God made them differently and with different needs. They cannot possibly live up to the unrealistic expectations placed on them. We can also do our sons a favor by not shouldering them with this expectation.

We need to give our daughters a reality check about marriage so they are not sorely disappointed. This will also prepare them for the fact that the euphoric feelings during dating and courtship will not last forever. It is not normal to ride the emotional high forever. Let's prepare them for the fact that their husbands, no matter how great they are, will not bring them ultimate happiness or fulfillment. When they learn to let go of this expectation, it frees them up to accept their men for who they are. Let's do our daughters a favor by teaching them that while they dream of their prince from a young age, their husbands will ultimately let them down at times. We have all been disappointed by our own princes, and we have disappointed them in return.

Appropriate Boundaries for Technology

If technology is a source of temptation for us, imagine what it is for our daughters. Our girls are growing up in an era we never experienced at their age. Texting, blogging, FaceTime, instant messaging, Instagram, Snapchat, chat rooms, and the Internet are the latest for this generation. They are introduced to new technology on a daily basis. Our girls have access to virtually anything through modern technology. This is where temptation starts. The things they pour into their hearts and minds can affect them for the rest of their lives, shaping the kind of women they become. Some things will stick in their minds forever.

Interestingly enough, most tweens and teenagers who own a cell phone do not use them for making phone calls. They use them for connecting in other ways. Clear and defined boundaries should be set for appropriate use of technology. Tell your daughter she is never to connect with an adult man (married or unmarried) on her cell phone. Do not assume she knows. In their naive minds, our daughters believe texting is simply a means to connect, and sometimes they will connect with anyone. Also set boundaries with photos and photo sharing. Instruct your daughter that no one should take a picture of her without her clothes on or in another compromising position. Teach her that she should not take pictures of herself and send them to the opposite sex because these pictures can easily be misinterpreted by young men. She should be taught not to respond to sexual comments on the Internet or cell phone. Emphasize to her that nothing really disappears on the Internet, even if she can no longer see it. Have her block senders who send inappropriate messages. Monitor her technology use periodically. Many parents are shocked to learn the content of the messages their kids receive from others. Some social media applications allow you to "follow" your daughter's account so you can see exactly what she posts and what gets posted by her friends.

Technology also tends to breed discontentment within young girls. Our daughters are mini versions of us, with the same fears and insecurities. Instant photos and "following friends" allow them to capture and view a friend's life at all times. Constantly viewing where a friend was and who she was with is not healthy or necessary. Being invited to every party or social event is unrealistic. Just as with adult women, there is also a level of boldness that is stirred within young girls through technology. Things are said through electronic devices that would never be said in person. It removes the element of propriety and "being a lady" that young girls should exhibit both with friends and with the opposite sex. This seems like common sense, but we cannot safely assume our girls know this. It is better to say something a hundred times and get an "I know, Mom," rather than to say nothing and to later hear a "Why didn't you tell me, Mom?"

To Stand for Her Marriage

I believe we also need to emphasize to our daughters that they will encounter problems in their marriages. When they encounter these problems, they need to fight for their husbands and their marriages. Teach them that they simply cannot call it quits just because their husbands are not living up to their expectations or meeting their needs. We need to model unconditional love to our daughters through our own marriages. Nothing is more powerful than a personal testimony they witness on how we handle marital issues. Share with your daughter your past struggles and what you learned from them. She should hear other women's stories of broken marriages and heartaches when poor choices were made. Let her see the ramifications of divorce and how it tears apart families and destroys the lives of children. Let's teach our girls that God places such a high value on the marriage covenant that He created it to be symbolic of the relationship between Christ and the church. He has promised to always love the church and to never leave her. We must constantly remind our daughters that God honors His covenants and requires us to do the same.

Our daughters watch, listen, and observe us. They know more than we realize and are very impressionable. There is no better person to model emotional purity for them than us. We are their examples. Since most girls turn into their mothers, we have an incredibly high responsibility. We must be women in pursuit of emotional purity not just for ourselves, but for our daughters as well.

Chapter 15

Give Up in Order to Gain

And you, my son Solomon, acknowledge the god of your father, and serve with wholehearted devotion and with a willing mind, for the Lord searches every heart and understands every desire and every thought. If you seek him, he will be found by you; but if you forsake him, he will reject you forever.

—*2 Chronicles 28:9*

Jezebel was the wife of King Ahab. Ahab was king over Israel for twenty-two years and did more evil than any other king before him. He married Jezebel, who was the daughter of the king of the Sidonians. The Sidonians were driven out by God during Joshua's time and were a people who had oppressed the Israelites. They worshipped idols, particularly Ashtoreth, the goddess of love and fertility. Ahab committed his own share of evil, but he was also influenced by his wife and the pagan gods she brought with her. At Mount Carmel, Jezebel watched God send His fire to consume a sacrifice saturated with water. Yet she still killed hundreds of the Lord's prophets. She also had Naboth unjustly accused and killed so Ahab could claim his vineyard.

Jezebel is also referred to in Revelation 2:20–23 in one of John's letters to the churches:

> Nevertheless, I have this against you: You tolerate that woman Jezebel, who calls herself a prophet. By her teaching she misleads my servants into sexual immorality and the eating of food sacrificed to idols. I have given her time to repent of her immorality, but she is unwilling. So I will cast her on a bed of suffering, and I will make those who commit adultery with her suffer intensely, unless they repent of her ways. I will strike her children dead. Then all the churches will know that I am he who searches hearts and minds, and I will repay each of you according to your deeds.

John is not referring to the same Jezebel who married King Ahab. The Jezebel he speaks of is a representation of the sensual and sexual idolatry that he accuses the church of tolerating. While the church was commended in certain areas, it tolerated sin. *Tolerate* is a strong word for us to pay attention to. As women, we can tolerate sin in our lives as well. Not practicing immorality is not enough. We must not tolerate immorality of any kind either.

God was patient with the church, giving them time to repent. He was clear that those who did not repent would suffer consequences. They needed to repent of tolerating Jezebel's ways. God is long-suffering and gives us time to repent of our ways as well. John also reminds the church that it is God who searches the heart and mind. God knew the inward sins the church was harboring and held them accountable for their secret sins. He holds us accountable for our secret sins as well.

Rahab lived in Jericho during the time Joshua sent two spies to inspect the land. She opened her home to the spies and hid them on her roof when the king's men came looking for them. By doing so, she jeopardized her own family's safety. She gave the spies refuge and refused to tell the king where they were. Rahab was a woman who had radically changed her ways. She acknowledged God as the one true God. Joshua 2:11 says, "For the Lord your God is God in heaven above and on the earth below." Rahab's change came from the inside out and radiated mightily when she was faced with danger. She welcomed the spies through faith and asked for protection for her family when the city was attacked. Rahab went on to marry Salmon, from the line of Abraham, and gave birth to Boaz. Her daughter-in-law was Ruth, a Moabitess. The Moabites were also enemies of the Israelites. However, Ruth turned from her gods to the one true God when she chose to follow Naomi, the mother of her deceased husband. Ruth married Boaz, and from their line came King David and eventually Jesus.

Both Jezebel and Rahab came from a long line of pagan worshippers, and both had a history of sin. Both women came face-to-face with the power of God and had a choice to make. Jezebel continued on in her destructive ways, which led to her demise and the end of her family line. Rahab chose very differently when she encountered God and turned from her sin. Her blessings came abundantly and continued on for generations, eventually giving way to the lineage of Christ. They both experienced God's miraculous deliverance and were given the opportunity to choose whom they would serve.

Jezebel's choices affected her and her children, and they ended her family line. Rahab's choices had a lasting impact on the generations that followed her. They were two very similar women who had two very different outcomes, all because of the choices they made.

Another story about choices is from the book of Exodus. God called the Israelites out of Egypt because He heard their groans and cries. The Egyptians had enslaved them and made their labor difficult and bitter. God used Moses to lead His people out of slavery. Even though they were being freed from the grips of Pharaoh, leaving their old lives behind wasn't easy. Their lives in Egypt may have been painful, but they were also comfortable and familiar lives. They left during the night with a sense of real urgency. They gathered what they could without even having time to prepare food for their long journey ahead (Exodus 12). They left for the promise of better lives in the land of Canaan. They left everything behind based on faith and moved forward solely guided by the word of God. The Israelites never saw the Promised Land due to their rebellion, but their children and grandchildren did. They left their old lives of bondage and slavery for the promise of freedom. They chose to give up in order to gain.

Giving up isn't always easy. Especially when it is a life we are accustomed to. Even bondage can become comfortable after time. Giving up also isn't easy if it is something we really want. It's hard and it's painful. It hurts to deny what our flesh craves and longs for. Often when we give something up, we lose other benefits associated with it. Severing an unhealthy friendship costs us a friend. Ending an inappropriate relationship with the opposite sex costs us conversation and connectedness.

Everything in life boils down to choices. Like Rahab and the Israelites, we need to willingly make choices on a daily basis. Sometimes the choices are big; sometimes they are small. It doesn't feel good to pass up the slice of cheesecake, especially when everyone else is having one. But we do it because we so desperately want to fit into the jeans or lose the last couple of pounds. We do it all in an effort to lose the weight. The outcome of the reward outweighs the cost for us. We need to put the same amount of effort into our emotional purity.

What would it take for you for the outcome to outweigh the cost? Only you can answer that question. What if you didn't have to do anything, but rather you had to give up something? What if you gave up all media-based entertainment filled with adultery and immorality for six months? This includes television, movies, magazines, books, social media, and unhealthy relationships. The world teaches us to do what feels good, looks good, and tastes good. God's standards are the complete opposite. Matthew 16:24 says, "Then Jesus said to his disciples, Whoever wants to be my disciple must deny themselves and take their cross and follow me." Jesus said if we are to follow Him, we must deny ourselves. We must deny ourselves the world's sinful pleasures that are harmful to our minds and emotions.

There is so much to gain when we clean up our thought lives. We will have more time to connect and communicate with our husbands. Our feelings won't be dictated by impure thoughts. Our lips will pour out love and kindness, and our actions will follow. In a perfect world, everything would flow in harmony because our hearts and minds would not be saturated with impurity. Although perfection isn't possible in this life, we strive toward holiness. Remember, evil begins in our minds. When our thought lives are clean, our lives match our thoughts, and our thoughts match our lives.

Over the next week, keep a running log of where and when you are confronted with impurity in your mind. You will see a pattern emerge, and then you may have a choice to make. You can either choose holiness for your mind, or you can continue to live in emotional darkness. Remember, it is not enough just to recognize evil. You must take action against evil as well. You will need to turn the channel, throw something out, or walk away. Holiness comes with a cost, but it also comes with a reward. I don't know your story or where you have been. But I do know that no matter what the situation, there is no shortage of grace. No sin is too great to turn from. God's love is great and overflowing, and His mercy never fails. No matter how far you have traveled, His love can reach you. No matter what you have done, His grace can transform you. Refuse to continue living paralyzed by your sins. Challenge yourself to give up in order to gain.

Chapter 16

Black and White

Above all else, guard your heart, for it is the wellspring of life.

—Proverbs 4:23

We have a reality that isn't part of any television show. Our reality is one that could never be depicted by the magic of Hollywood. It is uniquely ours and is constantly unfolding with no pause or stop buttons. We cannot press rewind or hit fast-forward. We cannot skip to our favorite parts and play them again. We can, however, choose to be completely immersed in our realities through our own marriages and families. When we invest in our realities, we are offered eternal rewards.

Psalm 45 is a wedding song and a beautiful description of the advice given to a bride as she waits for her king. It is a foreshadowing of the King that was to come, the Christ. The bride was counseled to forsake all others, giving full respect and adoration to her king. The king was captivated by her beauty and pure devotion. In giving her best to the king, she received blessings for generations to come. The message is clear. When we honor Christ, the blessings will come. They may not come immediately or in the manner we would like them to, but they will come. This is our hope. This is what we wait and strive for. Listen carefully to the promises given to the young bride in exchange for her pure adoration of the king.

> Listen, daughter, and pay careful attention: Forget your people and your father's house. Let the king be enthralled by your beauty; honor him, for he is your lord. The city of Tyre will come with a gift, people of wealth will seek your favor. All glorious is the princess within her chamber; her gown is interwoven with gold. In embroidered garments she is led to the king; her virgin companions follow her—those brought to be with her. Led in with joy and gladness, they enter the palace of the king.
>
> Your sons will take the place of your fathers; you will make them princes throughout the land.
>
> I will perpetuate your memory through all generations; therefore the nations will praise you for ever and ever. (Psalm 45:10–17)

We must stop defiling ourselves with what we allow to enter our minds. We are holy women, to be set apart in our speech, our actions, and our thoughts. We must not ride the wave of tolerance any longer, with one eye viewing immorality and the other in the pew. We must willfully and obediently choose what our eyes see and read and what we listen to every day. We need to step up and hold to God's standards for our emotional purity. We need to move beyond the stage of caring what others think and live as God commands us—as women living and breathing holiness. My hope and my prayer are that the Holy Spirit convicts where necessary and that you are moved toward a closer relationship with Jesus—not just a culture-driven, church-attending relationship, but an intimacy where you can love God with all your heart, soul, and mind.

Everything written here is because my own heart has been deeply convicted. I stand beside my sisters in this battle on a daily basis. Our emotional struggle will be a constant battle in this life. Do not be discouraged or give up hope if you find yourself going back to your fight against sin. Since we are human and flawed, our natural tendency will always be bent toward sin. Keep picking yourself up, keep reading and memorizing Scripture, and keep fighting for your emotional purity. Ephesians 6:12 says, "Our struggle is not against flesh and blood, but against the rulers, against the authorities, against the powers of this dark world, and against the spiritual forces of evil in the heavenly realm." The Enemy has waged war, and we must fight. We cannot give up or walk away. We are fighting, not just for our marriages and ourselves but for future generations. Even though the lure of sin will always be present, our appetite for it will decrease the less we feed it.

I leave you with my favorite verse, Proverbs 4:23: "Above all else, guard your heart, for it is the wellspring of life." Everything we do flows from our hearts, and we must protect them as if our very lives depend on it, because they do. Guard your heart with diligence, like a rare and beautiful jewel that has been gifted to you.

Handle your heart carefully, because it is fragile.
Protect it from theft, because it is valuable.
Hide it from darkness, because it is vulnerable.
Expose it to things that will enhance its beauty and brilliance.
Only then will your heart reflect light from every angle.

We have been given jewels and must choose to protect our hearts everyday with the choices we make. We honor God when we guard our hearts and our minds. God has called us to be women who have emotional purity. Please do not just take my word for things written here, read them for yourselves. Open the Bible, and you will discover amazing truths about loving God with all your heart, all your soul, and all your mind. You will discover there is no middle ground, no sitting on the fence, and no being lukewarm. With God, emotional purity is an all or nothing deal. It is black or white. There is nothing gray about it.

Appendix A

Dynamite

God's Word is powerful. Scripture says it is sharper than a double-edged sword cutting to the very core of the heart. Combining prayer with Scripture never comes back void and is a powerful weapon against the Enemy. It is like dynamite when thrown in the face of Satan. Following is a collection of dynamite:

- "Fix these words of mine in your hearts and minds; tie them as symbols on your hands and bind them on your foreheads. Teach them to your children, talking about them when you sit at home and when you walk along the road, when you lie down and when you get up" (Deuteronomy 11:18–19).
- "And you, my son Solomon, acknowledge the God of your father, and serve with wholehearted devotion and with a willing mind, for the Lord searches every heart and understands every desire and every thought. If you seek him, he will be found by you; but if you forsake him, he will reject you forever" (2 Chronicles 28:9).
- "Bring to an end the violence of the wicked and make the righteous secure—you, the righteous God who probes minds and hearts" (Psalm 7:9).

- "Test me, Lord, and try me, examine my heart and mind" (Psalm 26:2).
- "I will conduct the affairs of my house with a blameless heart. I will not look with approval on anything that is vile. I hate what faithless people do; I will have no part in it. The perverse of heart shall be far from me; I will have nothing to do with what is evil" (Psalm 101:3–4).
- "I have hidden your word in my heart that I might not sin against you" (Psalm 119:11).
- "Turn my heart toward your statutes and not toward selfish gain. Turn my eyes from worthless things; preserve my life according to your word" (Psalm 119:36–37).
- "Search me, God, and know my heart, test and know my anxious thoughts. See if there is any offensive way in me and lead me in the way of everlasting" (Psalm 139:23–24).
- "The Lord detests the thoughts of the wicked, but gracious words are pure in his sight" (Proverbs 15:26).
- "The highway of the upright avoids evil; those who guard their ways preserve their lives" (Proverbs 16:17).
- "Above all else, guard your heart, for it is the wellspring of life" (Proverbs 4:23).
- "You will keep in perfect peace those whose minds are steadfast, because they trust in you" (Isaiah 26:2).
- "Let the wicked forsake their ways and the unrighteous their thoughts. Let them turn to the Lord, and he will have mercy on them, and to our God, for he will freely pardon" (Isaiah 55:7).
- "Jerusalem, wash the evil from your heart and be saved. How long will you harbor wicked thoughts?" (Jeremiah 4:14).

- "But you, Lord Almighty, who judge righteously and test the heart and mind, let me see you vengeance on them, for to you I have committed my cause" (Jeremiah 11:20).
- "I the Lord search the heart and examine the mind, to reward each person according to their conduct, according to what their deeds deserve" (Jeremiah 17:10).
- "'This is the covenant I will make with the people of Israel after that time,' declares the Lord. 'I will put my law in their minds and write it on their hearts. I will be their God and they will be my people'" (Jeremiah 31:33).
- "Love the Lord your God with all your heart and with all your soul and with all your mind. This is the first and greatest commandment" (Matthew 22:37–38).
- "Those who live according to the flesh have their minds set on what the flesh desires, but those who live in accordance with the Spirit have their minds set on what the Spirit desires. The mind governed by the flesh is death, but the mind governed by the Spirit is life and peace. The mind governed by the flesh is hostile to God; it does not submit to God's law, nor can it do so. Those who are in the realm of the flesh cannot please God" (Romans 8:5–8).
- "Do not conform to the pattern of this world, but be transformed by the renewing of your mind. Then you will be able to test and approve what God's will is—his good, pleasing, and perfect will" (Romans 12:2).
- "Therefore, since we have these promises, dear friends, let us purify ourselves from everything that contaminates body and spirit, perfecting holiness out of reverence for God" (2 Corinthians 7:1).

- "We demolish arguments and every pretension that sets itself up against the knowledge of God, and take every thought captive to make it obedient to Christ" (2 Corinthians 10:5).
- "That, however, is not the way of life you learned when you heard about Christ and were taught in him accordance with the truth that is in Jesus. You were taught, with regard to your former way of life, to put off your old self, which is being corrupted by its deceitful desires, to be made new in the attitude of your minds, and to put on the new self, created to be like God in true righteousness and holiness" (Ephesians 4:20–24).
- "Since, then you have been raised with Christ, set your hearts on things above, where Christ is, seated at the right hand of God. Set your minds on things above, not on earthly things" (Colossians 3:1–2).
- "Therefore if you have any encouragement from being united with Christ, if any comfort from his love, if any common sharing in the Spirit, if any tenderness and compassion, then make my joy complete by being like-minded, having the same love, being one in spirit and of one mind" (Philippians 2:1–2).
- "And the peace of God, which transcends all understanding, will guard your hearts and minds in Christ Jesus. Finally brothers and sisters, whatever is true, whatever is noble, whatever is right, whatever is pure, whatever is lovely, whatever is admirable— if anything is excellent or praiseworthy—think about such things" (Philippians 4:7–8).
- "Therefore, holy brothers and sisters, who share in the heavenly calling, fix your thoughts on Jesus,

whom we acknowledge as our apostle and high priest" (Hebrews 3:1).

- "Make every effort to live at peace with everyone and to be holy; without holiness no one will see the Lord" (Hebrews 12:14).
- "Submit yourselves, then to God. Resist the devil, and he will flee from you. Come near to God and he will come near to you. Wash your hands, you sinners, and purify your hearts, you double-minded" (James 4:7–8).

Appendix B

Black and White Questions

An important step in our spiritual growth is to take action. We can read, study, and pray. But if we do nothing and take no action, then our reading, studying, and praying are in vain. It is not enough to merely recognize our sin. We must take the necessary steps to eliminate it from our lives. God desires us to be women who take action in our lives after our hearts are stirred.

On the following pages is a Bible study guide meant to facilitate discussion. Establish a safe and private atmosphere where you and other women preserve confidence. Some of the questions are difficult. They require an honest assessment of your emotional purity. Be willing to be vulnerable and transparent. God will use these moments. Be respectful to husbands and family members in your responses. Be open and willing to share because you are not the only one struggling.

Be willing to be flexible when you get off track. Hearts are vulnerable in moments of open and honest discussion, especially when someone is listening and truly cares. The questions are meant to facilitate sharing and not hinder it. Please be considerate and allow each woman to share her thoughts and responses. Always point to Scripture and trust God to do the convicting.

At the end of each week's set of questions, there is a real-life question: "What would you say or do if …?" They are called real-life questions because they are real scenarios that may happen or may have already happened to you. We often walk away from situations in our lives wishing we had handled them differently. The best way to handle them is to prepare for them before they occur. This allows us to set boundaries for ourselves before a compromising situation arises. We can answer confidently and stand our ground rather than be left fumbling for the right words. This also gives us an opportunity for discussion with our husbands. It allows us to establish boundaries each is comfortable with when dealing with the opposite sex. We cannot possibly prepare for every situation, but we can prepare our mindsets so that we respond in a Christ-like manner.

Be encouraged, and press on. I join you with other Christian sisters in this daily journey of emotional purity. With guarded hearts, we can truly love God with all our hearts, all our souls, and all our minds.

1: Appeal to the Audience

1. Read Matthew 14:13–14, Matthew 21:12–13, Mark 14:32–42, and John 11:17–37. Describe the emotion Jesus felt in each Scripture passage.
2. What preconceived ideas did you have about pornography?
3. When you first read the statistics on "Women in Pornography," did you think they applied to you? Why or why not?
4. What are the sources of pornography available in the daily life of women today? Which ones do you encounter most frequently?
5. Now that you understand pornography includes emotional impurity, how does this affect your answer to question 3?
6. Explain how pornography for most women is not sexual but emotional.
7. Read Ephesians 5:25–33. List the instructions given to husbands. Why do you think God gave husbands these instructions?
8. In what ways are a woman's emotions her greatest strength? Her greatest weakness?
9. Read Proverbs 4:23 in several different translations, including the *King James Version*, *The Good News Translation*, *The Living Bible*, *The Message*, and *The New Living Translation*. Share the different choices of words used to describe what the heart affects.

Real Life

What would you say or do if you started watching a movie with a group of girlfriends and a theme of adultery began unfolding?

2: Chick Flicks

1. Do you think there is a difference between a man being physically stimulated through inappropriate means and a woman being emotionally stimulated through inappropriate means? Why or why not?
2. Share an example where it is easy to cross over from feeling emotion to being emotionally satisfied. Is there anything from the entertainment world that emotionally satisfies you?
3. Do you think women are more easily deceived than men? Why or why not? Share a time when you were deceived about something but your husband was not. Did you recognize the deception at first? When did you finally become aware of it?
4. Read Psalm 44:20–22, Psalm 139:1–4, and Romans 2:15–16. What kinds of things does God specifically know?
5. Read Matthew 9:1–8. Which evil thoughts did Jesus address?
6. Is it comforting or frightening to understand what God knows about your thought life?
7. What kinds of things are easiest to hide from others but not from God?

Real Life

What would you say or do if a married man asked a question on your social media page? What if the married man slipped in a compliment to accompany the question?

3: In Our Hearts, in Our Minds, and in Our Marriages

1. Read Mark 7:20–23. How are the heart and the mind spiritually the same?
2. Explain the difference between having a sinful thought and feeding a sinful thought.
3. Read Matthew 12:34–35. What determines your speech?
4. Share a time when you have falsely convinced yourself of something.
5. What kind of things do you spend most of your thought life on? Share a time when your thoughts have controlled you physically and led to a behavior.
6. Read Philippians 4:7–9. Read aloud the attributes God instructs us to fill our minds with. Meditate on these eight attributes and take turns praying them over the women in your group.
7. Share examples of how you can fill your plate with vegetables (purity) instead of french fries (impurity).

Real Life

What would you say or do if a friend raved about a pornographic novel and offered you a copy to read?

4: Gray

1. Do you read the ingredient labels on foods? Do you read movie and book reviews for your children? How about for yourself?
2. Have you ever done something halfway? What was the outcome? If your children did something halfway, what would you tell them?
3. Why does God detest lukewarm? Why do you think it is such a struggle for women to be "all in" with their emotional lives?
4. Read Leviticus 19. Why did God command the Israelites to be "set apart"?
5. What are some things that specifically set you apart from the unbelieving world? Be specific, more than just "I go to church." Do you think people recognize you are different from them? Why or why not?
6. Read Philippians 4:8–9 and review the attributes God instructs us to fill our minds with. How do the things you view or read compare with these attributes?
7. Read Romans 13:12–14. What does Scripture say to clothe ourselves with?

Real Life

What would you say or do if you were with a group of women and they were inappropriately discussing someone's husband?

5: Holy Women: Part 1

1. Read 2 Timothy 3:1–9. What were the characteristics of the women who were taken advantage of? Do they have any similarities to women today? What were the characteristics of the ones who wormed their ways into homes?
2. What are some ways you can look at the entertainment world through God's standard of holiness?
3. Take a "service" inventory of the past month. Based on your inventory, are you feeding (serving) or consuming (being served) more?
4. How do you handle people who are consumed only with themselves?
5. Pray and ask God to give you a person you can minister to and serve. Share this person with your group.
6. Discuss some areas where women can easily be "romanced" outside their marriages.
7. Why is a hint of something so significant? Share a personal example of how a little bit can affect an outcome. Read Galatians 5:7–10. What example of a hint is used in this passage?

Real Life

What would you say or do if you saw a woman you knew well out to dinner with a man who wasn't her husband?

6: Holy Women: Part 2

1. Share a time when you became discontented in your own marriage as a direct result of what you heard, read, or witnessed in someone else's marriage. Read 1 Timothy 6:6–10 and Hebrews 13:5. What does God say about contentment?

2. Would others say you are a joy-filled or negative woman most of the time? Why? If you have no idea, ask a close and trusted friend. Read Psalm 126:1–3 and 1 Peter 1:3–9. What is the reason for us to have joy?

3. Share a time you have been consumed with a false reality. Did it affect you positively or negatively?

4. Where is it most difficult for you to be fruitful: in your actions, speech, or thought life? Why?

5. Do you see evidence of any sin in your life that may have been in the life of your mother or grandmother? What sin do you battle that you do not want your children or grandchildren to battle?

6. Do you recognize any tactics that Satan is already trying on your child? If so, what is your plan of action?

7. Share an area in your life where are you efficient. Are you just as efficient when you recognize temptation?

Real Life

What would you do if you found yourself becoming discontented while looking at pictures and posts on someone's social media page?

7: Traps and Lies

1. What have you entertained that could lead to a destructive path of believing "you deserve more or better than your husband has to offer"?
2. What is something your husband does well that you can be grateful for? Take a moment and thank God for those things your husband does well.
3. Everyone battles the thought that she may have married the wrong person at some point. What is something you can specifically do when this thought occurs?
4. Read Matthew 5:21–22 and 27–28. What does Jesus say about anger and lust?
5. Have you ever judged someone who committed a physical sin and realized you were guilty of the same sin in your heart?
6. If you are single, what areas do you struggle with most in protecting your emotional purity?
7. Which trap and lie is easiest for you to succumb to?

Real Life

What would you say or do if a man approached you and offered to buy you a drink while you were eating dinner with a girlfriend?

8: The Pretty Temptation

1. Read Matthew 4:1–11. In the first temptation, Satan appealed to Jesus' most basic need of hunger. What basic need does Satan continue to try to appeal to you with?
2. Share ordinary and good things that Satan often uses to tempt women.
3. Share any conditional lines you listen to. These conditional lines can be professional, financial, or marital.
4. What did Satan have to offer Jesus? What does Satan have to offer you?
5. Read Psalm 104. List the things God is in control of. Share an area of your life where you want control but recognize you have no control.
6. In the second and the third temptations, Satan tempted Jesus with promises of protection and power. How does Satan appeal to you in your need for protection? For power? Think in terms of control issues, marital issues, friendships, finances, careers, parenting, and education.
7. Share something Satan has lured you with that tastes good, looks good, and even feels good but has left you empty.
8. What can be a pretty temptation for women in television, social media, or even at a neighbor's house?

Real Life

Wha. would you say if you discovered a friend has a texting relationship with a married man?

9: Roller Coasters

1. Which roller coaster moments affect you most? Your menstrual cycle? Your husband? Loneliness, friends, media, literature, victories, or the normal moments? Have you noticed a pattern of when they typically affect you?
2. When the moment comes, what do you find yourself longing for? Think in terms of romance, communication, or friendship.
3. Do you find yourself longing to share or comment on social media constantly? Read Philippians 3:7–10. Where does our worth come from? Read 1 Peter 3:1–6 and 1 Timothy 3:11. What kind of woman is of great worth in God's eyes?
4. Take a moment to evaluate your friendships. What is your conversation centered on when you are with friends? Do you behave or speak differently with different friends (neighbors, colleagues, social media friends, friends from your past, other parents, church friends)?
5. Read Proverbs 12:26. Are your friends building you up or tearing you down emotionally and spiritually?
6. If you have unbelieving friends, do they influence you, or do you influence them? Which is easier, to influence or to be influenced? Does it depend on the situation?
7. Share a time when you have had to sever a friendship because of its negative influence on you. How did you feel when you severed it? Is there a friendship that you need to sever presently?
8. What is a boundary in your life you have neglected or failed to pay attention to?

Real Life

What would you say or do if you were invited to a bachelorette party for a close friend and learned a male stripper would be performing?

10: Guard Your Heart

1. Share a time you have been rude in the face of sin. How did others respond to your "rudeness"? Is there anything you need to be rude to presently?
2. Read Matthew 5:29–30. What parts of the body did Jesus say to throw out? Share something you need to throw out.
3. How would you respond if a friend confided in you that she was planning on divorcing her husband? Would her reason for divorcing matter to you?
4. Share a time when you have entertained Satan. Did you walk away with confusion or clarity?
5. Share a moment when your feelings followed your thoughts, whether positively or negatively. Do you usually respond to situations based on your feelings or God's truth?
6. Share an example from your own life when "practice makes permanent" has proven true. It can be a sport, a skill, or a daily task. Do not overlook the small things you do on a daily basis.
7. Who are you accountable to?

Real Life

What would you do if while reading a romance novel you found yourself emotionally satisfied by the love story?

11: Love Him for the Worst

1. Is there anything your child could do that would cause you to stop loving her? How about your husband?
2. What do you forgive others for repeatedly but not your husband? Why is it harder to forgive your husband for the same sin than it is to forgive someone else?
3. Read Matthew 18:21–35. How many times are we commanded to forgive? What is the measure of forgiveness that will be used with us? What is one thing specifically that you need to forgive your husband for without end?
4. Read Romans 2:1–6. When we judge others, what are we guilty of? What leads us to repentance?
5. Where do you need to be more vulnerable with your husband?

Real Life

What would you say or do if an old boyfriend contacted you to have lunch because he is in town?

12: Stake Your Marriage

1. When you first got married, what expectations did you have about your new husband? At what point did those expectations change?
2. Share a painful circumstance in your marriage through which you can still praise God. You may choose to do this silently.
3. Share something you have ownership of in your marriage. Read Ephesians 5:28–31.
4. In what ways are you specifically staking your marriage? Nothing is silly or insignificant. Remember, it is the small things that pave the way for the big things.
5. Share something that has lost its awe and wonder for you.
6. Read Isaiah 54. Name the promises God makes to His daughters.

Real Life

What would you do if after examining your wardrobe, you realized you had a different standard of modesty for church than you did for social settings with friends?

13: Women on a Rescue Mission

1. Have you ever had to confront a friend who was in sin? What was her reaction to you? Read Galatians 6:1–6. What is the scriptural way to approach a friend's sin?
2. Have you ever been confronted by anyone because of your sin? How did the person approach you? What was your reaction to the person?
3. Why do you think it is so hard for Christian women to confront someone in sin?
4. Do you think there is a difference between confronting a Christian and a non-Christian? What about a Christian you may know but don't have a relationship with?
5. Read Luke 17:3–4 and 2 Corinthians 2:5–11. How should we forgive and how often? What can happen to the offender when we choose not to forgive her?
6. Who do you need to forgive for hurting either you or someone you love?
7. In what way can you celebrate a friend who has overcome a struggle?
8. What are some ways women prey on the weaknesses of men? Of women? Personally reflect: is anything you do, say, or wear a stumbling block for a man?

Real Life

What would you say or do if you received an invitation to a sex toy party?

14: Guarding the Hearts of the Next Generation

1. What is something you wish your mother would have told you but didn't? How do you plan to do things differently with your daughter?
2. Why do you think physical purity is emphasized over emotional purity? Do you find it is easier to be physically pure or emotionally pure? Why?
3. What does God say about emotional purity for young girls? Read Psalm 119:9–16 and 1 Timothy 4:12.
4. Share areas in your life where your daughter observes you. Think of what you watch, what you read, and how and to whom you respond on social media.
5. If you are single or do not have a daughter, who is someone you can influence? Think of nieces, neighbors, babysitters, or a college girl you could mentor.

Real Life

What would you say or do if the discussion at a women's social turned toward the latest and most sexually explicit novel?

15: Give Up in Order to Gain

1. Read the story of Jezebel in 1 Kings 16:29–33, 18:4, 19:1–2, 21:1–25, and 2 Kings 9:22 and 30. What kind of woman was Jezebel? What did she tolerate? What kind of evil did she do?

2. Read Revelation 2:20–25. What did John accuse the church of? What does the word *tolerate* mean? What will happen to Jezebel's children?

3. Read Joshua 2:1. What kind of woman was Rahab formerly? Read Joshua 2:8–11. What happened that changed Rahab?

4. Read Matthew 1:1–6 and 16. Who did Rahab marry? Who came from her family line?

5. Read Exodus 12:31–39. Describe the conditions of the Israelites' exodus from Egypt. Do you think leaving Egypt was easy or difficult? Why?

6. Is it easier to give up something that's physical or emotional? Why?

7. Read Matthew 16:21–27. What had just occurred that prompted Jesus to say, "You must deny yourself"? Whose concerns did Peter have in mind? What does *deny* mean?

8. What are you willing to give up in order to gain? Based on what you give up, what will you specifically gain?

Real Life

What would you say or do if a married coworker of the opposite sex asked you to have lunch during the workday? Would it make a difference if you were married and he wasn't?

16: Black and White

1. Read the wedding song in Psalm 45. What attributes of God are listed? What is required of the bride? What promises are given to the bride? Do you believe these same promises are offered to you?
2. After going through this study, do you believe you need to protect your heart and mind?
3. On the following page, write down areas in which you need to guard your heart. There are three areas: "What I Watch," "What I Read," and "What and Whom I Listen To." Be specific in each area, including names of television shows, movies, social media sites, books, unhealthy relationships, and so on.

Real Life

What would you say or do if you found yourself becoming discontented with your husband and marriage after you watched a movie/show that featured grand romantic gestures?

Above all else, guard your heart, for it is the wellspring of life.

—*Proverbs 4:23*

What I Watch

_____
_____
_____
_____
_____

What I Read

_____
_____
_____
_____
_____

What and Whom I Listen To

_____
_____
_____
_____
_____

Appendix C

Kupendwa Ministries: A Reality Worth Investing In

With all the false and perceived realities we encounter, it is worthwhile to share a true reality. This is a reality the women of Jinja, Uganda, endure daily. Their reality is one of shame, hopelessness, and abandonment. Kupendwa Ministries is providing hope to these women both physically and spiritually. You can take part in the work Kupendwa is doing and minister to these women through your gifts and your prayers. Kupendwa Ministries is a reality worth investing in.

Kupendwa Ministries
Saving lives... Two at a time.

Kupendwa Ministries shares the gospel of Jesus Christ with mothers, babies, and their families in Uganda. Amy Washington is the founder and director of Kupendwa Ministries. Her passion and Kupendwa's mission is "Saving Lives … Two at a Time"— both physically and eternally.

Kupendwa's Crisis Pregnancy Maternity Home houses up to twenty desperately needy child and teen mothers along with their babies. Kupendwa educates, empowers, and enables these single young mothers to have bright futures. Kupendwa also distributes life-saving childbirth kits, provides services to mothers, and educates the communities on health, hygiene, sanitation, and childbirth topics.

There are many opportunities to support Kupendwa Ministries. You can sponsor a pregnant mother, provide childbirth kits, or provide educational support. If you feel led to help save two lives, please visit:

www.Kupendwaministries.org
kupendwaministries@gmail.com

Notes

1. Rachel B. Duke, "More women lured to pornography addiction." *The Washington Times.* July 11, 2010. *http://www.washingtontimes.com/ news/2010/jul/11/more-women-lured-to-pornography-addiction/* (March 31, 2014).

2. Rachel B Duke, "More women lured to pornography addiction." *The Washington Times.* July 11, 2010. *http://www.washingtontimes.com/news/2010/jul/11/ more-women-lured-to-pornography-addiction/* (March 31, 2014).

3. "Pornography." *Women's Services & Resources. https://wsr.byu.edu/ womenandpornography* (September 12, 2013).

4. Lindsay Goldwert, "Facebook named in a third of divorce filings in 2011." *New York Daily News.* Last updated May 24, 2012. *http://www.nydailynews.com/life-style/facebook-ruining-marriage-social-network-named-divorce-filings-2011-article-1.1083913* (March 13, 2014).

5. Richard Adams, "Facebook a top cause of relationship trouble, say US lawyers." *The Guardian.* March 8, 2011. *http://www.theguardian.com/ technology/2011/mar/08/facebook-us-divorces* (March 13, 2014).

6. "Hint." *Merriam-Webster.com. http://www.merriam-webster.com/dictionary/hint* (May 25, 2013).

7. "Associate." *NIV Study Bible.* 2002. (March 13, 2014).